antipasti

antipasti

GABRIELLA ROSSI

HERMES
HOUSE

For all recipes, **quantities** are given in both **metric** & **imperial** measures &, where appropriate, measures are also given in **standard cups** & **spoons**. Follow one set, but not a mixture, because they are **not interchangeable**.

Standard **spoon** & **cup measures** are level.
1 tsp = 5 ml, 1 tbsp = 15 ml, 1 cup = 250 ml/8 fl oz

Australian standard **tablespoons** are 20 ml. Australian readers should use 3 tsp in place of 1 tbsp for measuring small quantities of gelatine, cornflour, salt, etc.

Medium eggs are used unless otherwise stated.

This edition is published by Hermes House,

an imprint of Anness Publishing Ltd,
Hermes House, 88–89 Blackfriars Road, London SE1 8HA;
tel. 020 7401 2077; fax 020 7633 9499

www.hermeshouse.com; www.annesspublishing.com

If you like the images in this book and would like to investigate using them for publishing, promotions or advertising, please visit our website www.practicalpictures.com for more information.

Publisher Joanna Lorenz
Editor Charlotte Berman
Design Norma Martin
Production controller Don Campaniello
Recipes Angela Boggiano, Carla Capalbo, Jacqueline Clarke, Joanne Farrow, Silvana Franco, Nicola Graimes, Christine Ingram, Sara Lewis, Clare Lewis, Sunil Vijayakar, Steven Wheeler, Kate Whiteman, Jeni Wright
Photography Karl Adamson, Edward Allwright, Martin Brigdale, Michelle Garrett, Amanda Heyward, Janine Hosegood, David Jordan, Dave King, William Lingwood, Patrick McLeavey, Thomas Odulate

ETHICAL TRADING POLICY
At Anness Publishing we believe that business should be conducted in an ethical and ecologically sustainable way, with respect for the environment and a proper regard to the replacement of the natural resources we employ.
As a publisher, we use a lot of wood pulp to make high-quality paper for printing, and that wood commonly comes from spruce trees. We are therefore currently growing more than 500,000 trees in two Scottish forest plantations near Aberdeen – Berrymoss (130 hectares/320 acres) and West Touxhill (125 hectares/305 acres). The forests we manage contain twice the number of trees employed each year in paper-making for our books.
Because of this ongoing ecological investment programme, you, as our customer, can have the pleasure and reassurance of knowing that a tree is being cultivated on your behalf to naturally replace the materials used to make the book you are holding.
Our forestry programme is run in accordance with the UK Woodland Assurance Scheme (UKWAS) and will be certified by the internationally recognized Forest Stewardship Council (FSC). The FSC is a non-government organization dedicated to promoting responsible management of the world's forests. Certification ensures forests are managed in an environmentally sustainable and socially responsible basis. For further information about this scheme, go to www.annesspublishing.com/trees

antipasti

introduction

Start a meal in **style** with the freshest, brightest and **tastiest** sun-kissed **italian** recipes. Using ingredients that are native to italy and the mediterranean, such as **mozzarella**, tomatoes, basil, olive oil, prawns and **prosciutto** you can **create** a wealth of **simple** antipasti dishes that capture the intense **flavours, colours** and aromas of italy. classic recipes that have been passed down through generations of italians and **modern** twists on **regional** specialities combine to make this a **unique** collection of italian starters.

essential antipasti ingredients

WITH JUST A FEW **TRADITIONAL, FRESH INGREDIENTS**, SUCH AS **SUN-RIPENED** TOMATOES, PLUMP, **MOIST** MOZZARELLA AND **FRUITY** OLIVE OIL YOU CAN MAKE HUNDREDS OF COLOURFUL, **DELICIOUS** AND AUTHENTIC **ANTIPASTI.**

TOMATOES It is impossible to imagine antipasti without tomatoes; they crop up time and time again and are extremely versatile. Raw, vine-ripened plum tomatoes are delicious simply sliced and served with torn basil leaves and a drizzle of extra virgin olive oil, or roughly chopped as a topping for bruschetta. Slowly roasting tomatoes intensifies their flavour and makes them even more juicy, while soft, sun-dried tomatoes, which are available bottled in oil, have a distinct flavour of their own and can be used as they are, either sliced or chopped in sauces and salads.

AUBERGINES Because of their dense, satisfying texture aubergines are a good substitute for meat, and the deep purple colour of their skin enhances the appearances of many different antipasti. Although aubergines cannot be eaten raw, they can be grilled, roasted, fried, stuffed, stewed and even puréed, and they make a delicious partnership with mozzarella and tomatoes.

PEPPERS Yellow, orange, green and red peppers add a kaleidoscope of colour to antipasti. Green peppers are the least ripe of all, and are crunchier and less easy to digest than the mature red pepper, which has juicy, sweet flesh. All colours of pepper can be used in the same way, either raw in salads, roasted, stuffed and baked, or steamed. Peppers have a great affinity with olives, capers, aubergines, tomatoes and anchovies.

ONIONS Onions may not take centre stage as often as other vegetables, but they play a small but vital role in the majority of cooked antipasti dishes, as well as enlivening some uncooked ones. Vibrant deep red onions are particularly delicious raw, sliced thinly in salads. Small red and white onions can be stuffed with a Parmesan, breadcrumb and herb mixture, and then baked to make a mouthwatering hot appetizer. A selection of roast vegetables would not be complete without onions, and almost all soups rely on onions to provide depth of flavour.

GARLIC Like many Italian ingredients, this most pungent of vegetables is very good for you, topping the American National Cancer Institute's list as a potential cancer-preventative food. Garlic tastes and smells strongest when raw, when it is usually only used for rubbing on ciabatta slices to make bruschetta bases and as an ingredient of pesto. Finely sliced or crushed garlic softened gently in oil or butter is good in tomato sauces and soups, while mild roasted garlic can be spread directly on to grilled ciabatta.

PRAWNS There are so many varieties of prawn available in Italian coastal waters that it is almost impossible to recognize them all, but because they are all perfectly fresh each and every type makes delicious antipasti. Fresh prawns are usually boiled briefly, from 1 to 5 minutes depending on their size, or if large enough, grilled until they turn opaque, although they can also be fried and deep-fried. Cold prawns and artichokes on crostini make an elegant antipasti, while you won't forget the sight, taste or aroma of sizzling prawns, fried with chillies and garlic, served straight from the pan.

PROSCIUTTO Italy's famous salted and air-dried ham, that requires no cooking, owes its mild and sweet consistency partly to one of the ingredients fed to the pigs — whey from the local Parmesan-making process. Wafer-thin slices of this melt-in-the-mouth ham is best served simply, with melon or fresh figs, or rolled up with thin slices of veal and sage leaves to make saltimbocca.

ANCHOVIES Although you can buy fresh anchovies from specialist shops, they are more widely available preserved in salt or oil, oil-preserved anchovies having a better flavour. Anchovies add a important piquancy to many antipasti dishes, and are particularly good with cold roast vegetables and on crostini. Fresh anchovies are mild compared with the strong flavour of preserved anchovies, which should be used sparingly.

SALAMI There are dozens of types of salami produced in Italy, and while some are made from pure pork, others contain a myriad of ingredients, including beef, pepper, garlic, wine, fennel and paprika. Although it is never cooked, salami can regularly be found on the antipasti table, served simply with bread and cheese.

RICE Italy produces more rice, and a greater variety of rice, than anywhere else in Europe. The three types of short-grain risotto rice – Carnaroli, Arborio and Vialone Nano – have an unparalleled ability to absorb liquid and cook to a creamy softness while still retaining their shape. The best risottos, such as risotto alla Milanese, are classic Italian antipasti that are both delicious and extremely easy to make.

POLENTA A type of cornmeal made from ground maize, polenta is an adaptable staple from the north of Italy. Plain boiled polenta can be served on its own, or enriched with butter, and grilled polenta cut into triangles and spread with Gorgonzola is very tasty. Polenta can also be baked. Ready-to-slice polenta is available from most supermarkets.

MOZZARELLA Italian cooking could hardly survive without pure white egg-shaped mozzarella. The best variety of this delicate, silky-white cheese is made in the area around Naples using water buffalo's milk, and has a moist, springy texture and a deliciously milky flavour. The melting quality of mozzarella makes it perfect for grilled dishes, although it is equally delicious in salads.

PARMESAN Probably the most well-known Italian hard cheese, Parmesan can only be made in a strictly defined zone near Parma, and production methods have barely changed in 2,000 years. Parmigiano-Reggiano is the best Parmesan; it is aged for a minimum of two years and can be recognized by the word "Reggiano" stamped on the rind. A really good Parmesan is delicious served on its own in slivers or chunks, or with ripe pears and good red wine, and grated Parmesan enriches almost all cooked dishes.

BASIL More than any other herb, the pungent, intensely flavoured leaves of this plant are an essential ingredient in many Italian dishes, including the ubiquitous pesto. It also finds its way into soups, salads and almost all dishes associated with tomatoes, with which it has an extraordinary affinity. Sweet basil, with its bright green leaves, is the variety favoured by Italian cooks. This can be grown outside in sunny climates, or inside on the windowsill in more temperate climates.

BALSAMIC VINEGAR This must be the king of vinegars, so mellow and sweet that the best can be drunk on its own. Made in the area around Modena, genuine balsamic vinegar is strictly controlled by law and must have been aged in wooden barrels for between 12 and 50 years, by which time it has a slightly syrupy texture and a rich, deep mahogany colour. Balsamic vinegar is delicious as a dressing, even on its own, or as a marinade, especially for fish and seafood.

OLIVES AND OLIVE OIL Most of the olives cultivated in Italy are destined to be pressed into oil, but some are kept as table olives to be salted, pickled or marinated and served as antipasto. Green olives are unripe and have a sharper flavour than black olives, which continue to ripen on the tree and are not picked until later in the year. Black olives are used for making olive oil, the best of which is extra virgin, which is strictly controlled and regulated. Extra virgin olive oil is made by simply pressing the olives, with no further processing, leaving the oil with an acidity level of less than 1 per cent and a distinctive fruity flavour.

vegetables & cheese

ingredients

For the peppers

3 **red peppers**, skinned and
  seeded

3 **yellow peppers**, skinned and
  seeded

4 **garlic** cloves, sliced

handful of fresh **basil**, plus extra
  to garnish

extra virgin olive oil

salt and ground
  black pepper

For the mushrooms

450g/1lb **open
  cap mushrooms**

60ml/4 tbsp **extra virgin
  olive oil**

1 large **garlic** clove, crushed

15ml/1 tbsp chopped
  fresh **rosemary**

250ml/8fl oz/1 cup **dry
  white wine**

fresh **rosemary** sprigs, to garnish

For the olives

1 dried **red chilli**, crushed

grated rind of 1 **lemon**

120ml/4fl oz/½ cup **extra virgin
  olive oil**

225g/8oz/1⅓ cups **Italian
  black olives**

30ml/2 tbsp chopped fresh **flat
  leaf parsley**

1 **lemon** wedge, to serve

cook's tip

The pepper antipasto can be stored
in the fridge for up to 2 weeks
covered in olive oil in a screw-top jar.

marinated vegetables

SERVE THESE **TRADITIONAL** MARINATED
VEGETABLES IN ATTRACTIVE BOWLS WITH
GOOD ITALIAN **SALAMI**, THIN SLICES OF
PARMA HAM AND PLENTY OF FRESH
CRUSTY BREAD.

method

SERVES 6

1 Cut the peppers into strips lengthways and place them in a bowl with
   the sliced garlic and basil leaves. Add salt to taste, cover with oil and
   marinate for 3–4 hours before serving, tossing occasionally. When
   serving, garnish with more basil leaves.

2 Thickly slice the mushrooms and place in a large heatproof bowl. Heat
   the oil in a small pan and add the garlic and rosemary. Pour in the
   wine. Bring the mixture to the boil, then lower the heat and simmer for
   3 minutes. Add salt and pepper to taste.

3 Pour the mixture over the mushrooms. Mix well and leave until cool,
   stirring occasionally. Cover and marinate overnight. Serve at room
   temperature, garnished with rosemary sprigs.

4 Prepare the olives. Place the chilli and lemon rind in a small pan with
   the oil. Heat gently for about 3 minutes. Add the olives and heat for
   1 minute more. Tip into a bowl and leave to cool. Marinate overnight.
   Sprinkle the parsley over just before serving with the lemon wedge.

bean & rosemary bruschetta

THIS IS A **SOPHISTICATED** ITALIAN VERSION OF **BEANS ON TOAST**.

method

SERVES 12

1 Place the beans in a large bowl, cover with water and leave overnight. Drain and rinse the beans, then place in a saucepan and cover with fresh water. Bring to the boil and boil rapidly for 10 minutes. Reduce the heat and simmer for 50–60 minutes. Drain and set aside.

2 Meanwhile, place the tomatoes in a bowl and cover with boiling water Leave for 30 seconds, then peel, seed and chop the flesh. Heat the oil in a frying pan, add the fresh and sun-dried tomatoes, garlic and rosemary. Cook for 2 minutes until the tomatoes begin to break down and soften.

3 Add the tomato mixture to the cannellini beans, season to taste and mix well to combine.

4 Rub the cut sides of the bread slices with the garlic clove, then toast lightly. Spoon the cannellini bean mixture on top of the toast. Sprinkle with basil leaves and drizzle with a little extra olive oil before serving.

ingredients

150g/5oz/⅔ cup dried
   cannellini beans
5 **tomatoes**
45ml/3 tbsp **olive oil**, plus extra
   for drizzling
2 **sun-dried tomatoes** in oil,
   drained and finely chopped
1 **garlic** clove, crushed
30ml/2 tbsp chopped fresh
   rosemary
salt and ground **black pepper**
handful of fresh **basil** leaves,
   to garnish
12 slices Italian-style bread, such
   as **ciabatta**, to serve
1 large **garlic** clove, halved,
   to serve

ingredients

450g/1lb **cherry tomatoes**

For the pesto

90g/3½oz/1 cup fresh **basil**

3–4 **garlic** cloves

60ml/4 tbsp **pine nuts**

5ml/1 tsp **salt**, plus extra to taste

120ml/4fl oz/½ cup **olive oil**

45ml/3 tbsp freshly grated
   Parmesan cheese

90ml/6 tbsp freshly grated
   Pecorino cheese

ground **black pepper**

fresh **herb sprig**, to garnish

cherry tomatoes with pesto

THESE **MAKE** A **COLOURFUL** AND TASTY **APPETIZER** TO GO WITH **DRINKS**. MAKE THE **PESTO** WHEN FRESH BASIL IS **PLENTIFUL**, AND FREEZE IT IN **BATCHES**.

method
SERVES 10

1 Wash the tomatoes. Slice the top off each tomato, and carefully scoop out the seeds with a melon baller or small spoon.

2 Place the basil, garlic, pine nuts, salt and olive oil in a blender or food processor and process until smooth. Remove the contents to a bowl with a rubber spatula. If desired, the pesto may be frozen at this point, before the cheeses are added. To use when frozen, allow to thaw, then proceed to step 3.

3 Fold in the grated Parmesan and Pecorino cheeses (use all Parmesan if Pecorino is not available). Season with pepper, and more salt if necessary.

4 Use a small spoon to fill each tomato with a little pesto. Chill for about an hour before serving, and garnish with a fresh herb sprig.

grilled vegetable terrine

THIS **COLOURFUL** AND DELICIOUS LAYERED **TERRINE**, USES ALL THE **VEGETABLES** TRADITIONALLY ASSOCIATED WITH THE **MEDITERRANEAN**.

method

SERVES 8

1 Place the prepared red and yellow peppers skin side up under a hot grill and cook until the skins are blackened. Transfer to a bowl and cover with a plate. Leave to cool, then slice lengthways.

2 Arrange the aubergine and courgette slices on separate baking sheets. Brush them with a little oil and cook under the grill, turning them occasionally, until tender and golden.

3 Heat the remaining olive oil in a frying pan, and add the sliced onion, raisins, tomato purée and red wine vinegar. Cook gently until soft and syrupy. Leave to cool in the frying pan.

4 Line a 1.75 litre/3 pint/7½ cup terrine with clear film (it helps to lightly oil the terrine first), leaving a little hanging over the sides.

5 Pour half the tomato juice into a saucepan, and sprinkle with the gelatine. Dissolve gently over a low heat, stirring.

6 Place a layer of red peppers in the base of the terrine, and pour in enough of the tomato juice with gelatine to cover. Continue layering the aubergine, courgettes, yellow peppers and onion mixture, finishing with another layer of red peppers. Pour tomato juice over each layer.

7 Add the remaining tomato juice to any left in the pan, and pour into the terrine. Give it a sharp tap, to disperse the juice. Cover the terrine and chill until set.

8 To make the dressing, whisk together the oil and vinegar, and season. Turn out the terrine and remove the clear film. Serve in thick slices, drizzled with dressing. Garnish with basil leaves.

ingredients

2 large **red peppers**, quartered, cored and seeded

2 large **yellow peppers**, quartered, cored and seeded

1 large **aubergine**, sliced lengthways

2 large **courgettes**, sliced lengthways

90ml/6 tbsp **olive oil**

1 large **red onion**, thinly sliced

75g/3oz/½ cup **raisins**

15ml/1 tbsp **tomato purée**

15ml/1 tbsp **red wine vinegar**

400ml/14fl oz/1⅔ cups **tomato juice**

15g/½oz/2 tbsp **powdered gelatine**

fresh **basil leaves**, to garnish

For the dressing

90ml/6 tbsp **extra virgin olive oil**

30ml/2 tbsp **red wine vinegar**

salt and ground **black pepper**

ingredients

8 large **tomatoes**, firm and ripe

115g/4oz small **soup pasta**

8 **black olives**, stoned and
finely chopped

45ml/3 tbsp finely chopped mixed
fresh **herbs**, such as **chives**,
parsley, **basil** and **thyme**

60ml/4 tbsp grated
Parmesan cheese

60ml/4 tbsp **olive oil**

salt and ground **black pepper**

tomatoes with pasta stuffing

TOMATOES ARE ONE OF **ITALY'S** STAPLE FOODS, APPEARING IN MORE THAN **THREE-QUARTERS** OF ALL ITALIAN **SAVOURY** DISHES. THEY CAN BE **BAKED** WITH **VARIOUS STUFFINGS**. THIS ONE COMES FROM THE SOUTH.

method

SERVES 8

1 Wash the tomatoes, Slice off the tops, and scoop out the pulp with a small spoon. Chop the pulp and turn the tomatoes upside down on a rack to drain.

2 Place the pulp in a strainer, and allow the juices to drain off. Meanwhile, boil the pasta in a pan of boiling salted water. Drain it 2 minutes before the recommended cooking time elapses.

3 Preheat the oven to 190°C/375°F/Gas 5. Combine the pasta with the remaining ingredients in a bowl. Stir in the drained tomato pulp. Season with salt and pepper.

4 Stuff the tomatoes, and replace the tops. Arrange them in one layer in a well-oiled baking dish. Bake for 15–20 minutes. Peel off the skins, if desired. Serve hot or at room temperature.

roast garlic toasts

ROASTING GARLIC IN ITS **SKIN** ON A GRILL PRODUCES A SOFT, **AROMATIC PURÉE** WITH A **SWEET**, NUTTY **FLAVOUR** WHICH IS DELICIOUS **SPREAD** ON CRISP **TOAST.**

method

1 Slice the tops from the heads of garlic using a sharp kitchen knife.

2 Brush the garlic heads with extra virgin olive oil and add a few sprigs of fresh rosemary before wrapping in foil. Cook the foil parcels on a medium-hot grill for 25–30 minutes, turning occasionally, until the garlic is soft.

3 Slice the bread and brush each slice generously with olive oil. Toast the slices on the grill until crisp and golden, turning once.

4 Squeeze the garlic cloves from their skins on to the toasts. Sprinkle with the chopped fresh rosemary and olive oil, add salt and black pepper to taste.

ingredients

2 whole **garlic** heads
extra virgin olive oil
fresh **rosemary** sprigs
loaf of **ciabatta** or
thick **baguette**
chopped fresh **rosemary**
salt and ground
black pepper

mozzarella skewers

STACKS OF **FLAVOUR** – LAYERS OF **OVEN-BAKED** MOZZARELLA, **TOMATOES**, BASIL AND BREAD.

ingredients

12 slices thick white **bread**
45ml/3 tbsp **olive oil**
225g/8oz **mozzarella cheese**, cut into 5mm/¼in slices
3 plum **tomatoes**, cut into 5mm/¼in slices
15g/½oz/½ cup fresh **basil** leaves, plus extra to garnish
salt and ground **black pepper**
30ml/2 tbsp chopped fresh **flat leaf parsley**, to garnish

method

1 Preheat the oven to 220°C/425°F/Gas 7. Trim the crusts from the bread and cut each slice into four equal squares. Arrange on a baking sheet and brush on one side with half the olive oil. Bake for about 3–5 minutes until the squares are pale gold.

2 Remove from the oven and place the bread squares on a board with the other ingredients.

3 Make 16 stacks, each starting with a square of bread, then a slice of mozzarella topped with a slice of tomato and a basil leaf. Sprinkle with salt and pepper, then repeat, ending with the bread. Push a skewer through each stack and place on the baking sheet. Drizzle with the remaining oil and bake for 10–15 minutes until the cheese begins to melt. Garnish with fresh basil leaves and serve scattered with chopped fresh flat leaf parsley.

aubergine fritters

THESE **SIMPLY** DELICIOUS **FRITTERS** MAKE A SUPERB **VEGETARIAN** ANTIPASTO.

ingredients

1 large **aubergine**, about 675g/1½lb, cut into 1cm/½in thick slices
30ml/2 tbsp **olive oil**
1 **egg**, lightly beaten
2 **garlic** cloves, crushed
60 ml/4 tbsp chopped fresh **parsley**
130g/4½oz/2¼ cups fresh **white breadcrumbs**
90g/3½oz/generous 1 cup **feta cheese**, crumbled
45ml/3 tbsp plain **flour**
sunflower oil, for shallow frying
salt and ground **black pepper**

To serve
natural yogurt, flavoured with fried **red chillies** and **cumin seeds**
lime wedges

method

1 Preheat the oven to 190°C/375°F/Gas 5. Brush the aubergine slices with the olive oil, then place them on a baking sheet and bake for about 20 minutes until golden and tender. Chop the slices finely and place them in a bowl with the egg, garlic, parsley, breadcrumbs and feta. Add salt and pepper to taste, and mix well. Leave the mixture to rest for about 20 minutes. If the mixture looks very sloppy, add more breadcrumbs.

2 Divide the mixture into eight balls and flatten them slightly. Place the flour on a plate and season with salt and pepper. Coat the fritters in the flour, shaking off any excess.

3 Shallow fry the fritters in batches for 1 minute on each side, until golden brown. Drain on kitchen paper and serve with the flavoured yogurt and lime wedges for squeezing over.

ingredients

15ml/1 tbsp **lemon juice** or
  white wine vinegar
2 **globe artichokes**, trimmed
12 **garlic** cloves, unpeeled
45ml/3 tbsp **olive oil**
1 **lemon**
sea salt
sprigs of **flat leaf parsley**, to
  garnish

cook's tip
Artichokes are usually boiled, but
dry-heat cooking also works very
well. If you can get young artichokes,
try roasting them over a barbecue.

charred artichokes with lemon oil dip

THE **LEMON-FLAVOURED** DIP GIVES THE
SUCCULENT **ARTICHOKE** A REAL LIFT IN THIS
DELICIOUS STARTER.

method

SERVES 4

1 Preheat the oven to 200°C/400°F/Gas 6. Add the lemon juice or
vinegar to a bowl of cold water. Cut each artichoke lengthways into
wedges. Pull the hairy choke out from the centre of each wedge and
discard, then drop the artichokes into the acidulated water.

2 Drain the artichoke wedges and place in a roasting tin with the
garlic. Add the oil and toss well to coat. Sprinkle with salt and roast
for 40 minutes, stirring once or twice until they are tender and a
little charred.

3 Meanwhile, make the dip. Using a small, sharp knife thinly pare away
two strips of rind from the lemon. Lay the strips on a board and
carefully scrape away any remaining pith. Place the rind in a small pan
with water to cover. Bring to the boil, then simmer for 5 minutes. Drain
the rind, refresh it in cold water, then chop it roughly. Set aside.

4 Arrange the cooked artichokes on a serving plate and set aside to
cool for 5 minutes. Using the back of a fork, gently flatten the garlic
cloves so that the flesh squeezes out of the skins. Transfer the garlic
flesh to a bowl, mash to a purée then add the lemon rind. Squeeze
the juice from the lemon, then, using the fork whisk the olive oil from
the roasting tin and the lemon juice into the garlic mixture. Serve the
artichokes warm with the lemon dip, garnished with sprigs of parsley.

lemon & thyme stuffed mushrooms

PORTABELLO MUSHROOMS HAVE A **RICH** FLAVOUR AND A **MEATY TEXTURE** THAT GO WELL WITH THIS **FRAGRANT** HERB AND **LEMON STUFFING**, AND THE GARLICKY **PINE NUT** ACCOMPANIMENT.

method

SERVES 8

1 If using dried beans, soak them overnight, then drain and rinse well. Place in a saucepan, add enough water to cover and bring to the boil. Boil rapidly for 10 minutes, then reduce the heat, cook for 30 minutes until tender, then drain. If using canned beans, rinse, drain well, then set aside.

2 Preheat the oven to 200°C/400°F/Gas 6. Heat the oil in a large heavy-based frying pan, add the onion and garlic and sauté for 5 minutes until softened. Add the thyme and the mushroom stalks and cook for a further 3 minutes, stirring occasionally, until tender.

3 Stir in the beans, breadcrumbs and lemon juice, season well, then cook for 2 minutes until heated through. Mash two-thirds of the beans with a fork or potato masher, leaving the remaining beans whole.

4 Brush a baking dish and the base and sides of the mushrooms with oil, then top each one with a spoonful of the bean mixture. Place the mushrooms in the dish, cover with foil and bake for 20 minutes. Remove the foil. Top each mushroom with some of the goat's cheese and bake for a further 15 minutes, or until the cheese is melted and bubbly and the mushrooms are tender.

5 To make the pine nut tarator, place all the ingredients in a food processor or blender and process until smooth and creamy. Add more milk if the mixture appears too thick. Sprinkle with parsley, if using, and serve with the stuffed mushrooms.

ingredients

200g/7oz/1 cup dried or
   400g/14oz/2 cups drained,
   canned **aduki beans**
45ml/3 tbsp **olive oil**, plus extra
   for brushing
1 **onion**, finely chopped
2 **garlic** cloves, crushed
30ml/2 tbsp chopped fresh or
   5ml/1 tsp dried **thyme**
8 large **field mushrooms**, such as
   portabello mushrooms, stalks
   finely chopped
50g/2oz/1 cup fresh **wholemeal**
   breadcrumbs
juice of 1 **lemon**
185g/6½ oz/¾ cup **goat's**
   cheese, crumbled
salt and ground **black pepper**

For the pine nut tarator
50g/2oz/½ cup **pine**
   nuts, toasted
50g/2oz/1 cup cubed white **bread**
2 **garlic** cloves, chopped
200ml/7fl oz/scant 1 cup **milk**
45ml/3 tbsp **olive oil**
15ml/1 tbsp chopped fresh
   parsley, to garnish (optional)

ingredients

1kg/2¼lb **fennel bulbs**, washed
  and cut in half

50g/2oz/4 tbsp **butter**

40g/1½oz/⅓ cup freshly grated
  Parmesan cheese

baked fennel with parmesan cheese

FENNEL IS WIDELY EATEN IN ITALY, BOTH
RAW AND **COOKED**. IT IS DELICIOUS
MARRIED WITH THE **SHARPNESS** OF
PARMESAN **CHEESE** IN THIS **QUICK** AND
SIMPLE DISH.

method

SERVES 8

1 Cook the fennel in a large pan of boiling water until soft but not
   mushy. Drain. Preheat the oven to 200ºC/400ºF/Gas 6.

2 Cut the fennel bulbs lengthways into 4 or 6 pieces. Place them in a
   buttered baking dish.

3 Dot with butter. Sprinkle with the grated Parmesan. Bake in the
   hot oven until the cheese is golden brown, about 20 minutes.
   Serve at once.

variation
For a more substantial version of this dish, sprinkle 75g/3oz chopped ham over
the fennel before topping with the cheese.

fried mozzarella

THESE **CHEESE SLICES ORIGINATE** FROM THE **NEAPOLITAN** AREA, WHERE A LOT OF **MOZZARELLA** IS PRODUCED. THEY MUST BE MADE JUST BEFORE **SERVING.**

method

SERVES 2–3

1 Cut the mozzarella into slices about 1cm/½in thick. Gently pat off any excess moisture with kitchen paper.

2 Heat the oil until a small piece of bread sizzles as soon as it is dropped in (about 185ºC/360ºF). While the oil is heating beat the eggs in a shallow bowl. Spread some seasoned flour on one plate, and some breadcrumbs on another.

3 Press the cheese slices into the flour, coating them evenly with a thin layer of flour. Shake off any excess. Dip them into the egg, then into the breadcrumbs. Dip them once more into the egg, and then again into the breadcrumbs.

4 Fry immediately in the hot oil until golden brown. You may have to do this in two batches but do not let the breaded cheese wait for too long or the breadcrumb coating will separate from the cheese while it is being fried. Drain quickly on kitchen paper, and serve hot.

ingredients

300g/11oz **mozzarella cheese**
sunflower oil, for deep-frying
2 **eggs**
flour seasoned with **salt** and
  ground **black pepper**,
  for coating
dry white **breadcrumbs**,
  for coating

ingredients

1 loaf of **ciabatta**

60ml/4 tbsp **red pesto**

2 small **onions**

olive oil, for brushing

225g/8oz **mozzarella
  cheese**, sliced

8 **black olives**, halved
  and stoned

ciabatta toasts
with mozzarella

CIABATTA, A CRUSTY, **FLAVOURSOME**
ITALIAN BREAD, IS EVEN MORE **DELICIOUS**
WHEN MADE WITH **SPINACH**, SUN-DRIED
TOMATOES OR **OLIVES**. YOU CAN FIND THESE
VARIATIONS IN MANY **SUPERMARKETS.**

method

SERVES 8

1 Cut the bread in half horizontally and toast the cut sides lightly under
   the grill. Spread with pesto and keep warm.

2 Peel the onions and cut them horizontally into thin slices. Brush with oil
   and grill for 4–5 minutes, until caramelized.

3 Arrange the cheese slices on the bread. Add the onion slices and
   scatter some olives on top. Cut into slices. Return to the grill to melt
   the cheese then serve.

aubergine & mozzarella rolls

SLICES OF **GRILLED AUBERGINE** ARE STUFFED WITH SMOKED **MOZZARELLA**, **TOMATO** AND FRESH **BASIL** TO MAKE AN ATTRACTIVE **ANTIPASTO**. THE ROLLS ARE ALSO GOOD **BARBECUED**.

method

SERVES 8

1 Cut the aubergine lengthways into 10 thin slices and discard the two outermost slices. Sprinkle with salt and leave for 20 minutes. Rinse, then pat dry with kitchen paper.

2 Preheat the grill and line the rack with foil. Place the dried aubergine slices on the grill rack and brush liberally with oil. Grill for about 8–10 minutes until tender and golden, turning once.

3 Remove the aubergine slices from the grill, then place a slice of mozzarella and tomato and a basil leaf in the centre of each aubergine slice, and season to taste. Fold the aubergine over the filling and cook seam-side down under the grill until heated through and the mozzarella begins to melt. Serve drizzled with olive oil and a little balsamic vinegar, if using.

ingredients

1 large **aubergine**
45ml/3 tbsp **olive oil**, plus extra
    for drizzling (optional)
165g/5½oz **smoked mozzarella**
    cheese, cut into 8 slices
2 **plum tomatoes**, each cut into
    4 slices
8 large **basil** leaves
balsamic vinegar, for
    drizzling (optional)
salt and ground **black pepper**

ingredients

450g/1lb fresh leaf **spinach**,
   stalks trimmed
1 small **onion**, chopped
1 **garlic** clove, crushed
15ml/1tbsp **olive oil**
400g/14oz/1¾ cup
   ricotta cheese
75g/3oz/⅔ cup
   dried **breadcrumbs**
50g/2oz/½ cup plain **flour**
5ml/1tsp **Parmesan cheese**,
   freshly grated
fresh grated **nutmeg**, to taste
3 **eggs**, beaten
25g/1oz/2 tbsp **butter**, melted
salt and ground **black pepper**

For the sauce
1 large **red pepper**, chopped
1 small **red onion**, chopped
30ml/2 tbsp **olive oil**
400g/14oz can
   chopped tomatoes
good pinch of dried **oregano**
30ml/2 tbsp **single cream**

malfatti

IF YOU EVER FELT **DUMPLINGS** WERE A
LITTLE **HEAVY**, TRY MAKING THESE **LIGHT**
ITALIAN SPINACH AND RICOTTA **MALFATTI**
INSTEAD. SERVE THEM WITH A **SIMPLE**
TOMATO AND RED PEPPER **SAUCE**.

method   SERVES 6

1 Blanch the spinach until it is limp, then drain well in a sieve, pressing it
with the back of a ladle or spoon. Chop very finely.

2 Lightly fry the onion and garlic in the oil for 5 minutes then mix with
the spinach together with the ricotta, breadcrumbs, flour, salt, most of
the Parmesan and nutmeg.

3 Allow the mixture to cool, add the eggs and melted butter, then mould
into 12 small "sausage" shapes.

4 Meanwhile, make the sauce by lightly sautéeing the pepper and onion
in the oil for 5 minutes. Add the tomatoes, oregano and seasoning.
Bring to the boil then simmer for 5 minutes.

5 When cooked, remove from the pan and process to a pureé in a
blender or food processor. Return to the pan, then stir in the cream.
Check the seasoning.

6 Bring a shallow pan of salted water to a gentle boil and drop the
malfatti into it a few at a time and poach them for about 5 minutes.
Drain them well and keep warm.

7 Arrange the malfatti on warm plates and drizzle over the sauce. Serve
topped with the remaining Parmesan.

spinach & ricotta gnocchi

THE MIXTURE FOR THESE TASTY LITTLE **HERB DUMPLINGS** NEEDS TO BE HANDLED VERY **CAREFULLY** TO ACHIEVE **LIGHT** AND **FLUFFY** RESULTS. SERVE WITH A SAGE BUTTER AND GRATED PARMESAN.

method

SERVES 8

1 Cook the garlic cloves in boiling water for 4 minutes. Drain and pop out of the skins. Place in a food processor with the herbs and blend to a purée or mash the garlic with a fork and add the herbs to mix well.

2 Place the spinach in a large pan with just the water that clings to the leaves and cook gently until wilted. Leave to cool then squeeze out as much liquid as possible. Chop finely.

3 Place the ricotta in a bowl and beat in the egg yolk, spinach and garlic mixture. Stir in half the Parmesan, sift in the flour and mix well.

4 Using floured hands, break off pieces of the mixture slightly smaller than a walnut and roll into small dumplings.

5 Bring a large pan of salted water to the boil and carefully add the gnocchi. When they rise to the top of the pan they are cooked; this should take about 3 minutes.

6 The gnocchi should be light and fluffy all the way through. If not, simmer for a further minute. Drain well. Meanwhile, melt the butter in a frying pan and add the sage. Simmer gently for 1 minute. Add the gnocchi to the frying pan and toss in the butter over a gentle heat for 1 minute, then serve sprinkled with the remaining Parmesan.

ingredients

6 **garlic** cloves, unpeeled
25g/1oz mixed **fresh herbs**, such as **parsley**, **basil**, **thyme**, **coriander** and **chives**, finely chopped
225g/8oz **fresh spinach** leaves
250g/9oz/generous 1 cup **ricotta cheese**
1 **egg yolk**
50g/2oz/⅔ cup grated **Parmesan cheese**
75g/3oz/⅔ cup **plain flour**
50g/2oz/4 tbsp **butter**
30ml/2tbsp **fresh sage**, chopped
salt and ground **black pepper**

cook's tip
Squeeze the spinach dry to ensure the gnocchi are not wet and to give a lighter result. The mixture should be fairly soft and will be easier to handle if chilled for an hour before preparing the dumplings.

fish & seafood

ingredients

36 large **live mussels**, scrubbed
and bearded
105ml/7 tbsp **dry white wine**
60ml/4 tbsp finely chopped **fresh
flat leaf parsley**
1 **garlic clove**, finely chopped
30ml/2 tbsp fresh
white breadcrumbs
60ml/4 tbsp **olive oil**
chopped **fresh basil**, to garnish

crusty bread, to serve

For the pesto
2 fat **garlic cloves**, chopped
2.5ml/½ tsp **coarse salt**
100g/3¾oz/3 cups **basil leaves**
25g/1oz/⅓ cup **pine nuts,**
chopped
25g/1oz/⅓ cup freshly grated
Parmesan cheese
120ml/4fl oz/½ cup **extra virgin
olive oil**

gratin of mussels with pesto

THIS IS THE **PERFECT ANTIPASTO** FOR SERVING WHEN **TIME** IS **SHORT**, AS THE **PESTO** AND THE **MUSSELS** CAN BE **PREPARED** IN **ADVANCE**, AND THE DISH **ASSEMBLED** AND GRILLED AT THE LAST **MINUTE.**

method

SERVES 6

1 Put the mussels in a saucepan with the wine, clamp on the lid and shake over high heat for 3–4 minutes until the mussels have opened. Discard those which remain closed.

2 As soon as the mussels are cool enough to handle, remove them from the pan with a slotted spoon. Discard the empty half-shells. Strain the cooking liquid and keep it for another recipe. Arrange the mussels on their half-shells in a single layer in six individual gratin dishes, cover and set aside.

3 To make the pesto, put the chopped garlic and salt in a mortar and pound to a purée with a pestle. Then add the basil leaves and chopped pine nuts and crush to a thick paste. Work in the Parmesan cheese and gradually drip in enough olive oil to make a smooth and creamy paste. Alternatively, use a food processor.

4 Spoon the pesto over the mussels placed in gratin dish. Mix together the parsley, garlic and breadcrumbs. Sprinkle over the mussels, and drizzle with the oil.

5 Preheat the grill to high. Stand the dishes on a baking sheet and grill for 3 minutes. Garnish with chopped basil and serve with crusty bread.

> **cook's tip**
> Home-made pesto is best but when basil is out of season,
> or you are in a hurry, shop-bought pesto may be used instead.

marinated langoustines

FOR A REALLY **EXTRAVAGANT** TREAT, YOU COULD **MAKE** THIS WITH **MEDALLIONS** OF **LOBSTER**. FOR A **CHEAPER** VERSION, USE LARGE **PRAWNS**, ALLOWING SIX PER SERVING.

method

SERVES 8

1 Shell the langoustines and keep the discarded parts for making stock. Set aside.

2 Steam the asparagus over boiling salted water until just tender, but still a little crisp. Refresh under cold water, drain and place in a shallow dish.

3 Peel the carrots and cut into fine julienne shreds. Cook in a pan of lightly salted boiling water for about 3 minutes, until tender but still crunchy. Drain, refresh under cold water, drain again. Place in the dish with the asparagus.

4 Make the dressing. In a jug, whisk the tarragon vinegar with the oil. Season to taste. Pour over the asparagus and carrots and leave to marinate.

5 Heat the oil with the garlic in a frying pan until very hot. Add the langoustines and sauté quickly until just heated through. Discard the garlic.

6 Arrange the asparagus spears and the carrots on eight individual plates. Drizzle over the dressing left in the dish and top each portion with three langoustine tails. Top with the tarragon sprigs and scatter the chopped tarragon on top. Serve immediately.

ingredients

24 **langoustines**
24 fresh **asparagus spears**, trimmed
2 **carrots**
30ml/2 tbsp **olive oil**
1 **garlic** clove, peeled chopped
salt and ground **black pepper**
8 fresh **tarragon** sprigs and 15ml/1 tbsp chopped, to garnish

For the dressing
30ml/2 tbsp **tarragon vinegar**
120ml/4fl oz/½ cup **olive oil**

cook's tip
Most of the langoustines we buy have been cooked at sea, a necessary act because the flesh deteriorates rapidly after death. Bear this in mind when you cook the shellfish. Because it has already been cooked, it will only need to be lightly sautéed until heated through. If you are lucky enough to buy live langoustines, kill them quickly by immersing them in boiling water, then sauté until cooked through.

ingredients

16 large **mussels** or **clams**, in
their shells

4 large slices **bread**,
2.5cm/1in thick

40g/1½oz/3 tbsp **butter**

30ml/2 tbsp chopped
fresh **parsley**

1 **shallot**, very finely chopped

olive oil, for brushing

lemon wedges, to serve

crostini with
mussels & clams

IN THIS RECIPE, WHICH COMES FROM **GENOA**,
EACH **SEAFOOD CROSTINI** IS **TOPPED** WITH
A **MUSSEL OR CLAM** AND THEN **BAKED**.

method   SERVES 8

1 Wash the shellfish in several changes of water, then cut the "beards"
off the mussels, if using. Place the shellfish in a saucepan with a
cupful of water and heat until the shells open. (Discard any that do not
open.) As soon as they open, lift them out of the pan. Spoon out of
their shells, and set aside. Preheat the oven to 190ºC/375ºF/Gas 5.

2 Cut the crusts off the bread. Cut each slice into quarters. Scoop out a
hollow from the top of each piece large enough to hold a mussel or
clam. Do not cut right through.

3 Break the scooped-out bread into crumbs, and reserve. In a small
frying pan, heat the butter. Cook the parsley with the shallot and the
breadcrumbs until the shallot softens.

4 Brush each piece of bread with olive oil. Place a mussel or clam in
each hollow. Spoon a small amount of the parsley and shallot mixture
on to the molluscs. Place the crostini on an oiled baking sheet and
bake for 10 minutes. Serve at once, while still hot, with the lemon
wedges, for squeezing over.

stuffed roast peppers with pesto

SERVE THESE **SCALLOP-AND-PESTO**-FILLED **SWEET RED PEPPERS** WITH **ITALIAN** BREAD, SUCH AS **CIABATTA** OR **FOCACCIA**, TO MOP UP THE **GARLICKY** JUICES.

method

SERVES 8

1 Preheat the oven to 180°C/350°F/Gas 4. Cut the peppers in half lengthways, through their stalks. Scrape out and discard the cores and seeds. Wash the pepper shells and pat dry.

2 Put the peppers, cut-side up, in an oiled roasting tin. Divide the slivers of garlic equally among them and sprinkle with salt and pepper to taste. Spoon the oil into the peppers, then roast for 40 minutes.

3 Cut each of the shelled scallops in half to make two flat discs. Remove the peppers from the oven and place a scallop half in each pepper half. Top with pesto.

4 Return the tin to the oven and roast for 10 minutes more. Transfer the peppers to individual serving plates, sprinkle with grated Parmesan and garnish each plate with a few salad leaves and fresh basil sprigs. Serve warm.

---

cook's tip

Scallops are available from most fishmongers and supermarkets with fresh fish counters. Never cook scallops for longer than the time stated in the recipe or they will become tough and rubbery.

---

ingredients

4 squat **red peppers**
2 large **garlic** cloves, cut into
   thin slivers
60ml/4 tbsp **olive oil**
4 shelled **scallops**
45ml/3 tbsp **pesto**
salt and ground
   black pepper
salad leaves and fresh **basil**
   sprigs, to garnish
freshly grated **Parmesan**
   cheese, to serve

aromatic tiger prawns

THERE IS **NO ELEGANT WAY** TO EAT THESE **PRAWNS** – JUST **HOLD** THEM BY THE TAILS, **PULL** THEM OFF THE STICKS WITH YOUR FINGERS AND **POP** THEM INTO YOUR MOUTH.

ingredients

16 raw **tiger prawns**

2.5ml/½ tsp **chilli powder**

5ml/1 tsp **fennel seeds**

5 **Sichuan** or **black peppercorns**

1 **star anise**, broken into segments

1 **cinnamon stick**

30ml/2 tbsp **sunflower oil**

2 **garlic** cloves, chopped

2cm/¾in piece fresh **root ginger**, peeled and finely chopped

1 **shallot**, chopped

30ml/2 tbsp **water**

30ml/2 tbsp **rice vinegar**

30ml/2 tbsp **soft brown** or **palm sugar**

salt and ground **black pepper**

lime slices and chopped **spring onion**, to garnish

method

SERVES 8

1 Thread the prawns in pairs on eight wooden cocktail sticks. Set aside. Heat a frying pan, put in the chilli powder, fennel seeds, Sichuan or black peppercorns, star anise and cinnamon stick, broken into pieces, and dry-fry for 1–2 minutes to release the flavours. Leave to cool, then grind coarsely in a grinder or tip into a mortar and crush with a pestle.

2 Heat the sunflower oil in a shallow pan, add the garlic, ginger and chopped shallot and then fry gently until very lightly coloured. Add the crushed spices and seasoning and cook the mixture gently for 2 minutes. Pour in the water and simmer, stirring, for 5 minutes.

3 Add the rice vinegar and soft brown or palm sugar, stir until dissolved, then add the prawns. Cook for 3–5 minutes, until the seafood has turned pink, but is still very juicy. Serve hot, garnished with lime slices and spring onion.

---

cook's tip
If you buy whole prawns, remove the heads before cooking them.

---

prawn & vegetable crostini

USE **BOTTLED CARCIOFINI** (TINY **ARTICHOKE** HEARTS PRESERVED IN **OLIVE OIL**) FOR THIS SIMPLE **STARTER** WHICH CAN BE PREPARED VERY **QUICKLY**.

ingredients

450g/1lb unpeeled **cooked prawns**

4 thick slices of **ciabatta**, cut diagonally across

3 **garlic** cloves, peeled and 2 halved lengthways

60ml/4 tbsp olive oil

200g/7oz/2 cups small **button mushrooms**, trimmed

12 drained bottled **carciofini**

60ml/4 tbsp chopped **flat leaf parsley**

salt and ground **black pepper**

method

SERVES 4

1 Peel the prawns and remove the heads. Rub the ciabatta slices on both sides with the cut sides of the halved garlic cloves, drizzle with a little of the olive oil and toast in the oven or grill until lightly browned. Keep hot.

2 Finely chop the remaining garlic. Heat the remaining oil in a frying pan and gently fry the garlic until golden, but do not allow it to brown.

3 Add the mushrooms and stir to coat with oil. Season and sauté for about 2–3 minutes. Gently stir in the drained carciofini, then add the chopped flat leaf parsley.

4 Season again, then stir in the prawns and sauté briefly to warm through. Pile the prawn mixture on to the ciabatta. Pour over any remaining cooking juices and serve immediately.

---

cook's tip
Don't be tempted to use thawed frozen prawns, especially those that have been peeled. Freshly cooked prawns in their shells are infinitely nicer.

deep-fried prawns & squid

THE **ITALIAN** NAME FOR THIS RECIPE, **FRITTO MISTO**, MEANS "**MIXED FRY-UP**". ANY **MIXTURE** OF **SEAFOOD** CAN BE USED.

method

1 Make the batter in a large bowl by beating the egg whites, olive oil and vinegar together lightly with a wire whisk. Beat in the dry ingredients, and whisk until well blended. Beat in the water, a little at a time. Cover the bowl, and allow to stand for 15 minutes.

2 Heat the oil for deep-frying until a small piece of bread sizzles as soon as it is dropped in (about 185ºC/360ºF).

3 Dredge the prawns and squid pieces in the flour, shaking off any excess. Dip them quickly into the batter. Fry in small batches for about 1 minute, stirring with a draining spoon to keep them from sticking to each other.

4 Remove and drain on kitchen paper. Allow the oil to come back up to the correct temperature between batches. Sprinkle lightly with salt, and serve hot, with lemon wedges for squeezing over.

ingredients

vegetable oil, for deep-frying
600g/1lb 6oz medium **fresh prawns**, peeled and deveined
600g/1lb 6 oz **squid** (about 12 medium) cleaned and cut into bite-size pieces
115g/4oz/1 cup plain **flour**
salt
lemon wedges, to serve

For the batter
2 **egg whites**
30ml/2 tbsp **olive oil**
15ml/1 tbsp **white wine vinegar**
100g/3¾ oz/scant 1 cup **flour**
10ml/2 tsp **baking soda**
75g/3oz/⅓ cup **cornflour**
250ml/8fl oz/1 cup **water**

ingredients

2 **garlic** cloves, halved

25g/1oz/2 tbsp **butter**

1 small **red chilli**, seeded and
finely sliced

115g/4oz unpeeled, cooked
prawns, in the shell

sea salt and coarsely ground
black pepper

lime wedges, to serve

sizzling prawns

THIS DISH **WORKS** PARTICULARLY WELL WITH
TINY SHRIMPS WHICH CAN BE **EATEN**
WHOLE, BUT ANY TYPE OF UNPEELED
PRAWNS WILL BE **FINE**. **CHOOSE** A SMALL
FLAMEPROOF DISH OR FRYING **PAN** THAT
CAN BE TAKEN TO THE **TABLE** FOR SERVING
WHILE THE PRAWNS ARE STILL **SIZZLING**.

method

SERVES 4

1 Rub the cut surfaces of the garlic cloves over the base and sides of a
frying pan then throw them away. Add the butter to the pan and melt
over a fairly high heat until it just begins to turn golden brown.

2 Toss in the chilli and prawns. Stir-fry for 1–2 minutes until heated
through, then season to taste and serve with lime wedges for
squeezing over.

cook's tip
Wear gloves when handling chillies, or wash your hands thoroughly afterwards,
as the juices can cause severe irritation to sensitive skin, especially around the
eyes, nose or mouth.

ingredients

120ml/4fl oz/½ cup **olive oil**
finely grated rind and juice of
   1 large **lemon**
5ml/1 tsp crushed **chilli flakes**
350g/12oz **monkfish**
   fillet, cubed
350g/12oz **swordfish**
   fillet, cubed
350g/12oz thick **salmon** fillet
   or steak, cubed
2 **red**, **yellow** or **orange**
   peppers, cored, seeded and
   cut into squares
30ml/2 tbsp finely chopped fresh
   flat leaf parsley
salt and ground
   black pepper

**For the sweet tomato and
chilli salsa**
225g/8oz ripe **tomatoes**,
   finely chopped
1 **garlic** clove, crushed
1 fresh **red chilli**, seeded
   and chopped
45ml/3 tbsp **extra virgin
   olive oil**
15ml/1 tbsp **lemon** juice
15ml/1 tbsp finely chopped fresh
   flat leaf parsley
pinch of **sugar**

three-colour
fish kebabs

DON'T **MARINATE** THE FISH FOR MORE THAN AN **HOUR**, AS THE **FIBRES** OF THE FISH WILL BREAK DOWN AFTER THIS **TIME** AND IT WILL BE DIFFICULT NOT TO **OVERCOOK** IT.

method
SERVES 8

1 Put the oil in a shallow glass or china bowl and add the lemon rind and juice, the chilli flakes and pepper to taste. Whisk to combine, then add the fish chunks. Turn to coat evenly.

2 Add the pepper squares, stir, then cover and marinate in a cool place for 1 hour, turning occasionally.

3 Thread the fish and peppers on to eight oiled metal skewers, reserving the marinade. Barbecue or grill the skewered fish for 5–8 minutes, turning once.

4 Meanwhile, make the salsa by mixing all the ingredients in a bowl, and seasoning to taste with salt and pepper. Heat the reserved marinade in a small pan, remove from the heat and stir in the parsley, with salt and pepper to taste. Serve the kebabs hot, with the marinade spooned over, accompanied by the salsa.

salmon & scallop brochettes

WITH THEIR **DELICATE COLOURS** AND SUPERB **FLAVOUR**, THESE SKEWERS MAKE THE PERFECT **OPENER** FOR A **SOPHISTICATED** MEAL.

method

SERVES 8

1 Preheat the grill to medium-high. Cut off the top 7.5–10cm/3–4in of each lemon grass stalk. Reserve the bulb ends for another dish.

2 Cut the salmon fillet into 12 2cm/¾ in cubes. Thread the salmon, scallops, corals if available, onions and pepper squares on to the lemon grass and arrange the brochettes in a grill pan.

3 Melt the butter in a small pan, add the lemon juice and a pinch of paprika and then brush all over the brochettes. Grill the skewers for about 2–3 minutes on each side, turning and basting the brochettes every minute, until the fish and scallops are just cooked, but are still very juicy. Transfer to a platter and keep hot while you make the tarragon butter sauce.

4 Pour the dry vermouth and the leftover cooking juices from the brochettes into a small pan and boil fiercely to reduce by half. Add the butter and melt, then stir in the chopped fresh tarragon and salt and ground white pepper to taste. Pour the tarragon butter sauce over the brochettes and serve.

ingredients

8 **lemon grass** stalks

225g/8oz **salmon** fillet, skinned

8 **queen scallops**, with their corals if possible

8 **baby onions**, peeled and blanched

½ **yellow pepper**, cut into 8 squares

25g/1oz/2 tbsp **butter**

juice of ½ **lemon**

salt, ground **white pepper** and **paprika**

For the sauce

30ml/2 tbsp **dry vermouth**

50g/2oz/4 tbsp **butter**

5ml/1 tsp chopped fresh **tarragon**

ingredients

150ml/¼ pint/⅔ cup **milk**

115g/4oz/1 cup plain **flour**

450g/1lb **whitebait**

sunflower oil, for deep-frying

salt, ground **black pepper** and

cayenne pepper

devilled whitebait

SERVE THESE **DELICIOUSLY** CRISP **LITTLE FISH** WITH **LEMON WEDGES** AND THINLY SLICED **BROWN BREAD** AND BUTTER, AND EAT THEM WITH YOUR **FINGERS**.

method

SERVES 8

1 Put the milk in a shallow dish and spoon the flour into a polythene bag. Season the flour with salt, pepper and a little cayenne.

2 Dip a handful of the whitebait into the bowl of milk, drain them well, then pop them into the polythene bag. Shake gently to coat them evenly in the seasoned flour. Repeat until all the fish have been coated. This is the easiest method of flouring whitebait, but don't add too many at once, or they will stick together.

3 Heat the oil for deep-frying to 190°C/375°F or until a cube of stale bread, dropped into the oil, browns in 20 seconds. Add a batch of whitebait, preferably in a chip basket, and fry for 2–3 minutes, until crisp and golden brown. Drain and keep hot while you fry the rest. Sprinkle with more cayenne and serve very hot.

parmesan fish goujons

USE THIS **RECIPE**, WITH OR WITHOUT THE **CHEESE**, WHENEVER YOU FEEL LIKE **FRYING FISH**. THIS DISH IS LIGHT AND CRISP, JUST LIKE **FISH AND CHIP** SHOP BATTER.

method

SERVES 4

1 To make the cream sauce, mix the soured cream, mayonnaise, lemon rind, gherkins or capers, herbs and seasoning together, then chill.

2 To make the batter, sift the flour into a bowl. Mix in the other dry ingredients and salt.

3 Whisk in the egg yolk and milk to give a thick yet smooth batter. Then gradually whisk in 90ml/6 tbsp water. Season and leave to chill.

4 Skin the fish and cut into thin strips of similar length. Season the flour and then dip the fish lightly in the flour.

5 Heat at least 5cm/2in oil in a large pan with a lid. Whisk the egg white until stiff and gently fold into the batter until just blended.

6 Dip the floured fish into the batter, drain off any excess and then drop gently into the hot fat.

7 Cook the fish for 3–4 minutes, turning once, and cooking in batches so that the goujons don't stick to one another. When the batter is golden and crisp remove the fish with a draining spoon. Place on a kitchen-paper lined plate and keep warm in a low oven while cooking the rest.

8 Serve hot with the cream sauce, garnished with dill.

ingredients

375g/13oz **plaice** or **sole fillets**, or thicker fish such as **cod** or **haddock**
a little **flour**
oil, for deep-frying
salt and ground **black pepper**
springs of **dill**, to garnish

For the cream sauce
60ml/4 tbsp **soured cream**
60ml/4 tbsp **mayonnaise**
2.5ml/½ tsp grated **lemon rind**
30ml/2 tbsp chopped **gherkins** or **capers**
15ml/1 tbsp chopped, mixed fresh **herbs**, or 5ml/1 tsp dried

For the batter
75g/3oz/⅔ cup plain **flour**
25g/1oz/⅓ cup grated **Parmesan cheese**
5ml/1 tsp **bicarbonate of soda**
1 **egg**, separated
150ml/¼ pint/⅔ cup **milk**

poultry & meat

ingredients

4 **chicken breast** fillets, skinned

75g/3oz/1½ cups fresh
white breadcrumbs

40g/1½oz/½ cup **Parmesan
cheese**, finely grated

30ml/2 tbsp chopped
fresh **parsley**

2 **eggs**, beaten

100ml//3½fl oz/scant ½ cup
good-quality **mayonnaise**

100ml/3½fl oz/scant ½ cup
fromage frais

1–2 **garlic** cloves, crushed

50g/2oz/4 tbsp **butter**, melted

salt and ground **black pepper**

golden parmesan chicken

SERVED COLD WITH **GARLICKY** MAYONNAISE
THESE MORSELS OF **CHICKEN** MAKE A
GREAT STARTER.

method

SERVES 6

1 Cut each chicken fillet into six large chunks.

2 Mix together the breadcrumbs, Parmesan, parsley and seasoning in a shallow dish.

3 Dip the chicken pieces in the egg, then into the breadcrumb mixture. Place in a single layer on a baking sheet and chill for at least 30 minutes.

4 Meanwhile, to make the garlic mayonnaise, mix together the mayonnaise, fromage frais, garlic and pepper to taste. Spoon the mayonnaise into a small serving bowl. Chill until required.

5 Preheat the oven to 180ºC/350ºF/Gas 4. Drizzle the melted butter over the chicken pieces and cook for about 20 minutes, until crisp and golden. Serve the chicken immediately with the mayonnaise.

pan-fried chicken livers

THIS **FLORENTINE** DISH USES VIN SANTO, A SWEET DESSERT WINE FROM **TUSCANY**, BUT THIS IS NOT **ESSENTIAL**, AS ANY DESSERT WINE, OR A SWEET OR CREAM **SHERRY** WILL MAKE A GOOD SUBSTITUTE.

method

SERVES 6

1 Wash and dry the spinach and lollo rosso. Tear the leaves into a large pieces, season with salt and pepper to taste and toss gently to mix.

ingredients

75g/3oz fresh baby
 spinach leaves
75g/3oz **lollo rosso** leaves
75ml/5tbsp **olive oil**
15ml/1 tbsp **butter**
225g/8oz **chicken livers**,
 trimmed and thinly sliced
45ml/3 tbsp **vin santo**
salt and ground **black pepper**
50–75g/2–3oz fresh **Parmesan**
 cheese, shaved into curls,
to garnish

2 Heat 30ml/2 tbsp of the oil with the butter in a large heavy-based frying pan. When foaming, add the chicken livers and toss over a medium to high heat for 5 minutes or until the livers are browned on the outside but still pink in the centre. Remove from the heat.

3 Remove the livers from the pan with a slotted spoon, drain them on kitchen paper. Place the spinach, the lollo rosso and then the livers on individual plates.

4 Return the pan to a medium heat, add the remaining oil and the vin santo and stir until sizzling.

5 Pour the hot dressing over the leaves and livers and toss gently to coat. Sprinkle over the Parmesan shavings and serve at once.

ingredients

90ml/6 tbsp **olive oil**

45ml/3 tbsp fresh **lemon juice**

1 **garlic** clove, finely chopped

30ml/2 tbsp chopped fresh **basil**

2 **courgettes**

1 long, thin **aubergine**

300g/11oz boneless **turkey**, cut
    into 5cm/2in cubes

12–16 **pickled onions**

1 **red or yellow pepper**, cut
    into 5cm/2in squares

salt and ground
    black pepper

mediterranean turkey skewers

THESE SKEWERS ARE **EASY** TO ASSEMBLE, AND CAN BE COOKED ON A GRILL OR **BARBECUE.**

method

SERVES 4

1 In a small bowl mix the oil with the lemon juice, garlic and basil. Season with salt and pepper.

2 Slice the courgettes and aubergine lengthways into strips 5mm/¼ in thick. Cut them crossways about two-thirds of the way along their length. Discard the shorter length. Wrap half the turkey pieces with the courgette slices and the other half with the aubergine slices.

3 Prepare the skewers by alternating the turkey, onions and pepper pieces. Lay the prepared skewers on a platter and sprinkle with the flavoured oil. Leave to marinate for at least 30 minutes. Preheat the grill or prepare the barbecue.

4 Grill for about 10 minutes, turning the skewers occasionally. Serve hot.

grilled asparagus with prosciutto

THE MOST **FAMOUS** OF ITALY'S SALTED AND AIR-DRIED HAMS IS THE **EXCEPTIONALLY** MILD AND SWEET **PROSCIUTTO DI PARMA**, WHICH COMES FROM THE AREA AROUND **PARMA**. SERVE THIS ANTIPASTO WHEN FRESH **ASPARAGUS** IS PLENTIFUL AND NOT TOO PRICEY.

method

SERVES 4

1 Wash the asparagus thoroughly to remove any traces of grit.

2 Preheat the grill to high. Halve each slice of ham lengthways and wrap one half around each of the asparagus spears.

3 Brush the ham and asparagus lightly with oil and sprinkle with salt and pepper. Place on the grill rack. Grill for 5–6 minutes, turning frequently, until the asparagus is tender but still firm. Serve at once.

---
cook's tip
This dish will be particularly memorable if made with prosciutto di Parma, but if that is difficult to find any other prosciutto crudo will do.

---

ingredients

12 **asparagus** spears
6 slices of **prosciutto**
15ml/1 tbsp **olive oil**
sea salt and coarsely ground
   black pepper

ingredients

For the coating

225g/8oz/1⅓ cups
    prepared **farro**
1 **red chilli**, seeded and roughly
    chopped
1 **onion**, roughly chopped
salt and ground **black pepper**

For the stuffing

450g/1lb minced **lamb**
1 **onion**, finely chopped
50g/2oz/⅔ cup **pine nuts**
30ml/2 tbsp **olive oil**
7.5ml/1½ tsp ground **allspice**
60ml/4 tbsp chopped fresh
    coriander
sunflower oil for deep frying

To serve

avocado slices and
    coriander sprigs

deep-fried lamb patties

THIS DISH IS MADE WITH **FARRO** WHEAT, WHICH IS **RARELY** EATEN OUTSIDE **TUSCANY**. IT MUST BE BOILED FOR UP TO 3 HOURS BEFORE IT IS READY TO **EAT**.

method   SERVES 6

1 Divide the minced meat into two equal portions.

2 Process the farro in the blender or food processor with the chilli, onion, half the meat and plenty of salt and pepper.

3 Fry the remaining onion and pine nuts in the oil for 5 minutes. Add the allspice and remaining minced meat and fry gently, breaking up the meat with a wooden spoon, until browned. Stir in the coriander and seasoning.

4 Turn the coating mixture out on to a work surface and shape into a cake. Cut into 12 wedges.

5 Flatten one piece and spoon some stuffing into the centre. Bring the edges of the coating up over the stuffing, ensuring that the filling is completely encased.

6 Heat oil to a depth of 5cm/2in a large pan until a few coating crumbs sizzle on the surface.

7 Lower half of the filled patties into the oil and fry for about 5 minutes until golden. Drain on kitchen paper and keep them hot while cooking the remainder. Serve with avocado slices and coriander sprigs.

mushrooms stuffed with prosciutto

MAKE SURE THE FIELD **MUSHROOMS** ARE REALLY **FRESH**. THEIR SKINS SHOULD BE **UNBLEMISHED** AND THEIR EDGES INTACT.

method

SERVES 8

1 Preheat the oven to 190°C/375ºF/Gas 5. Fry the onion gently in half the butter for 6–8 minutes until soft but not coloured.

2 Meanwhile, break off the stems of the field mushrooms, setting the caps aside. Drain the dried mushrooms and chop these and the stems of the field mushrooms finely. Add to the onion together with the garlic and cook for a further 2–3 minutes.

3 Transfer the mixture to a bowl, add the breadcrumbs, egg, herbs and seasoning. Melt the remaining butter in a small pan and generously brush over the mushroom caps. Arrange the mushrooms on a baking sheet and spoon in the filling. Bake in the oven for 20–25 minutes until well browned.

4 Top each with a strip of prosciutto, garnish with parsley and serve.

ingredients

1 **onion**, chopped

75g/3oz/6 tbsp unsalted **butter**

8 field **mushrooms**

15g/½oz/¼ cup dried **ceps**, **bay boletus** or **saffron milk-caps**, soaked in warm water for 20 minutes

1 **garlic** clove, crushed

75g/3oz/¾ cup fresh white **breadcrumbs**

1 **egg**

75ml/5 tbsp chopped fresh **parsley**

15ml/1 tbsp chopped fresh **thyme**

salt and ground **black pepper**

115g/4oz **prosciutto di Parma or San Daniele,** thinly sliced

fresh **parsley**, to garnish

ingredients

1 **garlic** clove, peeled and cut
   in half

1½ **lemons**

50ml/2fl oz/¼ cup **extra virgin
   olive oil**

2 bunches **rocket**

4 very thin slices of **beef**
   top round

115g/4oz **Parmesan cheese**,
   thinly shaved

salt and ground
   black pepper

carpaccio
with rocket

CARPACCIO IS A **FINE** DISH OF RAW BEEF
MARINATED IN LEMON JUICE AND OLIVE
OIL. IT IS **TRADITIONALLY** SERVED WITH
FLAKES OF FRESH PARMESAN CHEESE. USE
VERY **FRESH** MEAT OF THE BEST **QUALITY**.

method

SERVES 4

1 Rub a small bowl all over with the cut side of the garlic. Squeeze the
lemons into the bowl. Whisk in the olive oil. Season with salt and
pepper. Allow the sauce to stand for at least 15 minutes before using.

2 Carefully wash the rocket and tear off any thick stalks. Spin or pat dry.
Arrange the rocket around the edge of a serving platter, or divide
among individual plates.

3 Place the beef in the centre of the platter, and pour on the sauce,
spreading it evenly over the meat. Arrange the shaved Parmesan on
top of the meat slices. Serve at once.

saltimbocca

THESE ROLLS ARE SO **GOOD** THAT, AS THEIR ITALIAN NAME IMPLIES, THEY **"JUMP INTO YOUR MOUTH".**

method

SERVES 8

1 Gently pound the veal slices with a mallet until thin. Lay a piece of prosciutto over each slice. Top with a sage leaf, and season.

2 Roll the escalopes around the filling and secure each roll with a wooden cocktail stick.

3 Heat half the butter in a frying pan just large enough to hold the rolls in one layer. When the butter is bubbling add the veal, turning the rolls to brown them on all sides. Cook for about 7–10 minutes, or until the veal is cooked. Remove to a warmed plate.

4 Add the remaining butter and the hot broth or stock to the frying pan, and bring to the boil, scraping up the brown residue on the base of the pan with a wooden spoon. Pour the sauce over the veal rolls, and serve.

ingredients

8 small **veal** escalopes

8 small slices **prosciutto**

8 fresh **sage** leaves

40g/1½oz/3 tbsp **butter**

120ml/4fl oz/½ cup **meat broth** or **stock**

salt and ground **black pepper**

meat-stuffed cabbage rolls

STUFFED CABBAGE LEAVES ARE **EASY** TO MAKE, AND A **GOOD** WAY OF USING UP COOKED MEATS.

ingredients

1 head **Savoy cabbage**
75g/3oz **white bread**
milk, for soaking bread
350g/12oz/2 cups very finely
    chopped cold meat, or fresh
    minced lean **beef**
1 **egg**
30ml/2 tbsp finely chopped
    fresh **parsley**
1 **garlic** clove, finely chopped
50g/2oz/⅔ cup freshly grated
    Parmesan cheese
nutmeg, salt and ground
    black pepper
75ml/5 tbsp **olive oil**
1 **onion**, finely chopped
250ml/8fl oz/1 cup **dry
    white wine**

method

1 Cut the leaves from the cabbage. Save the innermost part for soup. Blanch the leaves a few at a time in a large pan of boiling water for 4–5 minutes. Refresh under cold water. Spread the leaves out on clean dish towels to dry.

2 Cut the crusts from the bread and discard. Soak the bread in a little milk for about 5 minutes. Squeeze out the excess moisture with your hands.

3 In a mixing bowl combine the chopped or minced meat with the egg and soaked bread. Stir in the parsley, garlic and Parmesan. Season with nutmeg, salt and pepper.

4 Divide any very large cabbage leaves in half, discarding the rib. Lay the leaves out on a flat surface. Form little sausage-shape mounds of stuffing, and place them at the edge of each leaf. Roll up the leaves, tucking the ends in as you roll. Squeeze each roll lightly in the palm of your hand to help the leaves to stick.

5 In a large, shallow, flameproof casserole or deep frying pan large enough to hold all the cabbage rolls in one layer, heat the olive oil. Add the onion, and cook gently until it softens. Raise the heat slightly, and add the cabbage rolls, turning them over carefully with a large spoon as they begin to cook.

6 Pour in half the wine. Cook over a low to moderate heat until the wine has evaporated. Add the rest of the wine, cover the pan, and cook for 10–15 minutes more. Remove the lid, and cook until all the liquid has evaporated. Remove from the heat, and allow to rest for about 5 minutes before serving.

polpettes with mozzarella & tomato

THESE ITALIAN **MEATBALLS** ARE MADE WITH BEEF AND **TOPPED** WITH MOZZARELLA **CHEESE** AND TOMATO.

ingredients

½ slice **white bread**,
 crusts removed
45ml/3 tbsp **milk**
675g/1½lb minced **beef**
1 **egg**, beaten
50g/2oz/⅔ cup
 dry **breadcrumbs**
vegetable oil, for frying
2 beefsteak or other large
 tomatoes, sliced
15ml/1 tbsp chopped fresh
 oregano
1 **mozzarella cheese**, cut into
 8 slices
8 drained canned **anchovies**, cut
 in half lengthways
salt and ground **black pepper**

method

SERVES 8

1 Preheat the oven to 200°C/400°F/Gas 6. Put the bread and milk into a small saucepan and heat very gently, until the bread absorbs all the milk. Mash it to a pulp and leave to cool.

2 Put the beef into a bowl with the bread mixture and the egg and season with salt and pepper. Mix well, then shape the mixture into eight patties. Sprinkle the breadcrumbs on to a plate and dredge the patties, coating them thoroughly.

3 Heat about 5mm/¼in oil in a large frying pan. Add the patties and fry for 2 minutes on each side, until brown. Transfer to a greased ovenproof dish, in a single layer.

4 Lay a slice of tomato on top of each patty, sprinkle with oregano and season with salt and pepper. Place the mozzarella slices on top. Arrange two strips of anchovy, placed in a cross on top of each slice of mozzarella.

5 Bake for 10–15 minutes, until the mozzarella has melted. Serve hot, straight from the dish.

rice & polenta

ingredients

275g/10oz/1½ cups plain
risotto, prepared according to
instructions on packet

75g/3oz/1 cup
Parmesan cheese

3 **eggs**

breadcrumbs and plain **flour**,
to coat

115g/4oz/⅔ cup **mozzarella**
cheese, cut into small cubes

oil, for deep-frying

dressed curly **endive** and **cherry
tomatoes**, to serve

rice balls with mozzarella

THESE **DEEP-FRIED** BALLS OF RISOTTO GO
BY THE NAME OF **SUPPLI AL TELEFONO** IN
THEIR NATIVE ITALY. **STUFFED** WITH
MOZZARELLA CHEESE, THEY ARE VERY
POPULAR **SNACKS**.

method

SERVES 6

1 Put the just-cooked risotto in a bowl, stir in the Parmesan cheese and allow it to cool completely. When cold, beat two of the eggs, and stir them into the risotto until well mixed.

2 Use your hands to form the rice mixture into balls the size of a large egg. If the mixture is too moist to hold its shape well, stir in a few tablespoonfuls of breadcrumbs. Poke a hole into the centre of each ball with your finger, then fill it with a few small cubes of mozzarella, and close the hole over again with the rice mixture.

3 Heat the oil for deep-frying until a small piece of bread sizzles as soon as it is dropped in.

4 Spread some flour on a plate. Beat the remaining egg in a shallow bowl. Sprinkle another plate with breadcrumbs. Roll the balls in the flour, then in the egg, and finally in the breadcrumbs.

5 Fry them a few at a time in the hot oil until golden and crisp. Drain on kitchen paper while the remaining balls are being fried. Serve hot, with a simple salad of dressed curly endive leaves and cherry tomatoes.

mini rice omelettes

THESE **DELIGHTFUL** LITTLE **OMELETTES** CAN BE MADE WITH **LEFTOVER** RICE.

method

SERVES 4

1 Heat half the olive oil in a large frying pan and stir-fry the rice, with the potato, spring onions and garlic, over a high heat for 3 minutes until golden.

2 Tip the rice and vegetable mixture into a bowl and stir in the parsley and eggs, with plenty of salt and pepper. Mix well.

3 Heat the remaining oil in the frying pan and drop in large spoonfuls of the rice mixture, leaving room for spreading. Cook the omelettes for 1–2 minutes on one side then flip over and cook the other side.

4 Drain the omelettes on kitchen paper and keep hot while cooking the remaining mixture to make 8 small omelettes in all. Serve hot.

ingredients

30ml/2 tbsp **olive oil**

115g/4oz/1 cup cooked **white rice**

1 **potato**, grated

4 **spring onions**, thinly sliced

1 **garlic** clove, finely chopped

15ml/1 tbsp chopped fresh **parsley**

3 **eggs**, beaten

salt and ground **black pepper**

ingredients

1 **aubergine**

1 large **green pepper**

2 large **tomatoes**

1 large **onion**, chopped

2 **garlic** cloves, crushed

45ml/3 tbsp **olive oil**, plus extra
 for sprinkling

200g/7oz/1 cup **brown rice**

600ml/1 pint/2½ cups
 vegetable stock

75g/3oz/⅔ cup **pine nuts**

50g/2oz/⅓ cup **currants**

45ml/3 tbsp chopped fresh **dill**

45ml/3 tbsp chopped
 fresh **parsley**

15ml/1 tbsp chopped fresh **mint**

salt and ground
 black pepper

natural **yogurt** and **dill** sprigs
 to serve

rice-stuffed vegetables

VEGETABLES SUCH AS PEPPERS MAKE **WONDERFUL** CONTAINERS FOR **SAVOURY** FILLINGS. INSTEAD OF STICKING TO ONE TYPE OF VEGETABLE SERVE A **SELECTION**. THICK, CREAMY YOGURT IS THE **IDEAL** ACCOMPANIMENT FOR THEM.

method

SERVES 6

1 Halve the aubergine, scoop out the flesh with a sharp knife and chop finely. Salt the insides and leave to drain upside down for 20 minutes.

2 Meanwhile, halve the pepper, then seed and core. Cut the tops from the tomatoes, scoop out the insides and chop roughly along with the tomato tops. Set the tomato shells aside. Fry the onion, garlic and chopped aubergine in the oil for 10 minutes, then stir in the rice and cook for two minutes. Add the tomato flesh, stock, pine nuts, currants and seasoning. Bring to the boil, cover and lower the heat. Simmer for 15 minutes then stir in the herbs.

3 Preheat the oven to 190°C/375°F/Gas 5. Blanch the aubergine and green pepper halves in boiling water for about 3 minutes, then drain them upside down on kitchen paper.

4 Spoon the rice filling into all six vegetable containers and place on a lightly greased shallow baking dish. Drizzle some olive oil over the stuffed vegetables and bake for 25–30 minutes. Serve hot, topped with spoonfuls of yogurt and dill sprigs.

rice cakes with dolcelatte

FOR A REALLY **IMPRESSIVE** ANTIPASTO,
SERVE THESE RICE CAKES TOPPED
WITH GARLIC **MAYONNAISE** AND
SALT-CURED **SALMON**.

method

SERVES 6

1 Remove the stalk, leaves and choke to leave just the heart of the artichoke; chop the heart finely.

2 Melt the butter in a saucepan and gently fry the chopped artichoke heart, onion and garlic for 5 minutes until softened.

3 Add the rice and cook for about 1 minute, stirring occasionally, until the rice grains are glossy.

4 Keeping the heat fairly high, gradually add the stock, stirring constantly until all the liquid has been absorbed and the rice is cooked – this should take about 20 minutes. Season well, then stir in the Parmesan. Transfer to a bowl. Leave to cool, then cover and chill for at least 2 hours.

5 Spoon about 15ml/1 tbsp of the mixture into the palm of one hand, flatten slightly, and place a few pieces of diced cheese in the centre. Shape the rice around the cheese to make a small ball. Flatten slightly then roll in the polenta, shaking off any excess. Repeat with the remaining mixture to make about 12 cakes.

6 Shallow-fry in hot olive oil for 4–5 minutes until the rice cakes are crisp and golden brown. Drain on kitchen paper and serve hot, garnished with flat leaf parsley.

ingredients

1 **globe artichoke**
50g/2oz/¼ cup **butter**
1 small **onion,** finely chopped
1 **garlic** clove, finely chopped
115g/4oz/⅔ cup **risotto rice**
450ml/¾ pint/scant 2 cups hot
   chicken stock
50g/2oz/⅔ cup freshly grated
   Parmesan cheese
150g/5oz **Dolcelatte**
   cheese, diced
45–60ml/3–4 tbsp fine **polenta**
olive oil, for frying
salt and ground **black pepper**
flat leaf **parsley**, to garnish

cook's tip
Fresh Parmesan should be piquant, grainy and not so hard that it is difficult to grate.

ingredients

225g/8oz **broccoli,** cut into very
    small florets
1 **onion,** chopped
2 **garlic** cloves, crushed
1 large **yellow pepper,** sliced
30ml/2 tbsp **olive oil**
50g/2oz/¼ cup **butter**
225g/8oz/1¼ cups **risotto rice**
120ml/4fl oz/½ cup **dry**
    white wine
300ml/¼ pint/1¼ cups **stock**
oil, for greasing
115g/4oz **Pecorino or**
    Parmesan cheese
4 **eggs**, separated
salt and ground **black pepper**
sliced **tomato** and chopped
    parsley, to garnish

broccoli risotto torte

LIKE A SPANISH **OMELETTE**, THIS IS A
SAVOURY CAKE SERVED IN **WEDGES**. IT IS
GOOD COLD OR HOT, AND NEEDS ONLY A
SALAD **GARNISH** AS AN ACCOMPANIMENT.

method

SERVES 8

1 Blanch the broccoli for 3 minutes then drain and reserve.

2 In a large saucepan, gently fry the onion, garlic and pepper in the oil
and butter for 5 minutes until they are soft. Stir in the rice, cook for a
minute then pour in the wine. Cook, stirring the mixture until the liquid
is absorbed.

3 Pour in the stock, season well, bring to the boil then lower to a
simmer. Cook for 20 minutes, stirring occasionally.

4 Meanwhile, grease a 25cm/10in round deep cake tin and line the
base with a disc of greaseproof paper. Preheat the oven to
180°C/350°F/Gas 4.

5 Stir the cheese into the rice, allow the mixture to cool for 5 minutes,
then beat in the egg yolks and stir in the broccoli.

6 Whisk the egg whites until they form soft peaks and carefully fold into
the rice mixture. Turn into the prepared tin and bake for about 1 hour
until risen, golden brown and slightly wobbly in the centre.

7 Allow the torte to cool in the tin, then chill if serving cold. Run a knife
around the tin and shake out on to a serving plate. If liked, garnish
with sliced tomato and chopped parsley.

fried tomatoes with polenta crust

THE **CONTRAST** BETWEEN THE **SWEET** AND JUICY **TOMATOES** AND THE **CRUNCHY** POLENTA CRUST IN THIS UNUSUAL DISH IS BOTH **SURPRISING** AND **DELICIOUS**.

method

SERVES 4

1 Cut the tomatoes into thick slices. Mix the polenta or cornmeal with the oregano and garlic powder.

2 Put the flour, egg and polenta or cornmeal into different bowls. Dip the tomato slices in the flour, then in the beaten egg and finally into the polenta.

3 Fill a shallow frying pan one third full of oil and heat steadily until quite hot.

4 Slip the tomato slices into the oil carefully, a few at a time, and fry on one side until crisp. Remove and drain. Repeat with the remaining tomatoes, reheating the oil in between. Serve with salad.

ingredients

4 large, firm, underripe **tomatoes**
25g/8oz/1 cup **polenta** or
    coarse cornmeal
5ml/1 tsp dried **oregano**
2.5ml/½ tsp **garlic** powder
plain **flour**, for dredging
1 **egg**, beaten with seasoning
sunflower oil, for deep-frying

grilled polenta with gorgonzola

GRILLED **POLENTA** IS DELICIOUS, AND IS A GOOD WAY OF USING UP **COLD** POLENTA. TRY IT WITH ANY SOFT **FLAVOURSOME** CHEESE.

method

SERVES 8

1 Bring the water to the boil in a large heavy-based saucepan. Add the salt. Reduce the heat to a simmer, and begin to add the polenta flour in a fine rain. Stir constantly with a whisk until the polenta has all been incorporated.

2 Switch to a long-handled wooden spoon, and continue to stir the polenta over a low to moderate heat for about 10 minutes, or until it is a thick mass, and pulls away from the sides of the pan. For best results, never stop stirring the polenta until you remove it from the heat.

3 When the polenta is cooked, sprinkle a work surface or large board with a little water. Spread the polenta out on to the surface in a layer 2cm/¾in thick. Allow to cool completely. Preheat the grill.

4 Cut the polenta into triangles. Grill until hot and speckled with brown on both sides. Spread with the Gorgonzola or other cheese. Serve immediately.

ingredients

1.5 litres/2½ pints/
   6¼ cups **water**
15ml/1 tbsp **salt**
225g/8oz/1 cup **polenta**
350g/12oz/2½ cups **Gorgonzola**
   or other **cheese**, at room
   temperature

ingredients

750ml/1¼ pints/3 cups **stock**
   or **water**
5ml/1 tsp **salt**
225g/8oz/1 cup **polenta**
25g/1oz/2 tbsp **butter**
65g/2½oz/5 tbsp mixed chopped
   fresh **parsley**, **chives** and
   basil, plus extra to garnish
olive oil, for brushing
4 large **plum** or **beef**
   tomatoes, halved
salt and ground
   black pepper

herb polenta

GOLDEN **POLENTA** MADE WITH FRESH
SUMMER HERBS AND SERVED WITH GRILLED
TOMATOES MAKES A TASTY ANTIPASTO.

method   SERVES 8

1 Place the stock or water in a saucepan, with the salt, and bring to the
boil. Reduce the heat and stir in the polenta.

2 Stir constantly over a moderate heat for about 10 minutes, or until the
polenta begins to thicken and come away from the sides of the
saucepan.

3 Remove from the heat and stir in the butter, chopped herbs
and pepper.

4 Lightly grease a wide pan or dish and pour the polenta into it,
spreading it evenly. Set aside until cool and set.

5 Turn out the polenta and cut into squares or stamp out rounds with a
large biscuit cutter. Brush with olive oil. Lightly brush the tomatoes
with oil and sprinkle with salt and pepper. Cook the tomatoes and
polenta under a medium-hot grill for about 5 minutes, turning once.
Serve garnished with fresh herbs.

ingredients

50g/2oz/¼ cup **butter**, plus extra
   for greasing
250ml/8fl oz/1 cup **milk**
450g/16oz/2 cups
   polenta
115g/4oz/1 cup grated
   mozzarella cheese
115g/4oz/1 cup crumbled **torta
   di Dolcelatte cheese**,
2 **garlic** cloves, roughly chopped
a few fresh **sage** leaves, chopped
salt and ground
   black pepper
prosciutto, to serve

cook's tip
Pour the polenta into the boiling
liquid in a continuous stream, stirring
constantly with a wooden spoon or
balloon whisk. If using a whisk,
change to a wooden spoon once the
polenta thickens.

polenta elisa

THIS DISH COMES FROM THE **VALLEY**
AROUND **LAKE COMO**. IT MAKES A
DELICIOUS ANTIPASTO, WITH A MIXED
SALAD AND SOME SLICED **SALAMI**
OR **PROSCIUTTO**.

method

SERVES 8

1 Preheat the oven to 200°C/400°F/Gas 6. Lightly butter a
20–25cm/8–10in baking dish.

2 Bring the milk and 750ml/1¼ pints/3 cups water to the boil in a large
saucepan, add 5ml/1 tsp salt, then tip in the polenta. Cook for about
10 minutes or according to the instructions on the packet.

3 Spoon half the polenta into the baking dish and level. Cover with half
the grated mozzarella and crumbled Dolcelatte. Spoon the remaining
polenta evenly over the top and sprinkle with the remaining cheeses.

4 Melt the butter in a small saucepan until foaming, add the garlic and
sage and fry, stirring, until the butter turns golden brown.

5 Drizzle the butter mixture over the polenta and cheese and grind black
pepper liberally over the top. Bake for 5 minutes. Serve hot, with
slices of prosciutto.

polenta & salami balls

A POPULAR **SNACK** FOOD, THE **POLENTA** BALLS IN THIS RECIPE CONTAIN **BITE-SIZED** PIECES OF SALAMI, BUT **CHUNKS** OF **SMOKED HAM** OR CHEESE ARE EQUALLY SUITABLE AS AN ALTERNATIVE.

method

SERVES 8

1 Stir the polenta and water together in a heavy-based saucepan. Bring to the boil and, stirring all the time, cook for 10 minutes, or until suitable for rolling into balls. Stir in the butter and season well.

2 With lightly floured hands roll the balls to double the size of a walnut and place the salami in the middle before rolling up.

3 Fry the balls in the oil at 180–190°C/350–375°F, for 2–3 minutes or until golden brown. Drain well on kitchen paper. Serve with pan-fried tomatoes and chopped herbs.

ingredients

225g/8oz/generous 2 cups **polenta**
600ml/1 pint/2½ cups lightly salted **water**
generous knob of **butter**
115g/4oz/1 cup roughly chopped **salami**,
sunflower oil, for deep-frying
salt and ground **black pepper**
pan-fried **tomatoes** and chopped fresh **herbs**, to serve

salads

fennel, orange & rocket salad

THIS LIGHT AND **REFRESHING** SALAD IS IDEAL TO SERVE BEFORE **SPICY** OR RICH FOODS.

ingredients

2 **oranges**
1 **fennel** bulb
115g/4oz **rocket** leaves
50g/2oz/⅓ cup **black olives**

For the dressing
30ml/2 tbsp extra virgin **olive oil**
15ml/1 tbsp **balsamic vinegar**
1 small **garlic** clove, crushed
salt and ground **black pepper**

method

1 With a vegetable peeler, cut strips of rind from the oranges, leaving the pith behind and cut into thin julienne strips. Cook in boiling water for a few minutes. Drain. Peel the oranges, removing all the white pith. Slice them into thin rounds and discard any pips.

2 Cut the fennel bulb in half lengthways and slice across the bulb as thinly as possible, preferably in a food processor fitted with a slicing disc or using a mandoline.

3 Combine the oranges and fennel in a serving bowl and toss with the rocket leaves.

4 Mix together the oil, vinegar, garlic and seasoning and pour over the salad, toss together well and leave to stand for a few minutes. Sprinkle with the black olives and julienne strips of orange.

aubergine, lemon & caper salad

THIS COOKED VEGETABLE RELISH IS A **CLASSIC** SICILIAN DISH, WHICH IS **DELICIOUS** SERVED AS AN ACCOMPANIMENT TO COLD MEATS, OR SIMPLY ON ITS OWN WITH SOME GOOD **CRUSTY** BREAD. MAKE SURE THE AUBERGINE IS WELL COOKED UNTIL IT IS **MELTINGLY** SOFT.

ingredients

1 large **aubergine**, about
    675g/1½lb
60ml/4 tbsp **olive oil**
grated **rind** and **juice** of
    1 **lemon**
30ml/2 tbsp **capers**, rinsed
12 stoned **green olives**
30ml/2 tbsp chopped fresh
    flat leaf **parsley**
salt and ground
    black pepper

method

1 Cut the aubergine into 2.5cm/1in cubes. Heat the olive oil in a large frying pan and cook the aubergine cubes over a medium heat for about 10 minutes, tossing regularly, until golden and softened. You may need to do this in two batches. Drain on kitchen paper and sprinkle with a little salt.

2 Place the aubergine cubes in a large serving bowl, toss with the lemon rind and juice, the capers, olives and chopped parsley and season well with salt and pepper. Serve at room temperature.

---
cook's tip
This will taste even better when made the day before. It will store, covered in the fridge, for up to 4 days. To enrich this dish, add toasted pine nuts and shavings of Parmesan cheese. Serve with crusty bread.

ingredients

olive oil, for brushing

1 large **red onion**,
    cut into wedges

300g/11oz ready-made **polenta,**
    cut into 1cm/½in cubes

225g/8oz baby **spinach** leaves

1 **avocado**, peeled, stoned
    and sliced

5ml/1 tsp **lemon juice**

For the dressing

60ml/4 tbsp extra virgin
    olive oil

juice of ½ **lemon**

salt and freshly ground
    black pepper

avocado, red onion & spinach salad

THE **SIMPLE** LEMON DRESSING GIVES A SHARP **TANG** TO CREAMY AVOCADO, SWEET RED ONIONS AND CRISP SPINACH. **GOLDEN** POLENTA CROUTONS, WITH THEIR **CRUNCHY** GOLDEN EXTERIOR AND SOFT CENTRE, ADD A **DELICIOUS** CONTRAST.

method   SERVES 4

1 Preheat the oven to 200°C/400°F/Gas 6. Brush the onion wedges and polenta cubes with oil and bake until the onion is tender and the polenta is crisp and golden, turning them regularly to prevent sticking.

2 Meanwhile, make the dressing. Place the olive oil, lemon juice and seasoning to taste in a bowl or screw–top jar. Stir or shake thoroughly to combine.

3 Place the baby spinach leaves in a serving bowl. Toss the avocado slices in the lemon juice to prevent them browning, then add to the spinach with the roasted onions.

4 Pour the dressing over the salad and toss gently to combine. Sprinkle the polenta croûtons on top or hand them around separately and serve immediately.

---
cook's tip
If you can't find ready-made polenta you can make your own using instant polenta grains. Simply cook according to the packet instructions, then pour into a tray and leave to cool and set.
---

panzanella salad

OPEN-TEXTURED, **ITALIAN-STYLE** BREAD IS ESSENTIAL FOR THIS **COLOURFUL**, CLASSIC TUSCAN SALAD.

ingredients

10 slices thick day-old
   Italian-style bread
1 **cucumber**, peeled and
   cut into chunks
5 **tomatoes**, seeded and diced
1 large **red onion**, chopped
200g/7oz/1⅓ cups **black olives**
20 **basil** leaves

For the dressing
60 ml/4 tbsp extra virgin
   olive oil
15ml/1 tbsp **red** or **white**
   wine vinegar
salt and ground
   black pepper

method

SERVES 6

1 Soak the bread in water for about 2 minutes, then lift out and squeeze gently, first with your hands and then in a dish towel to remove any excess water. Chill for 1 hour.

2 Meanwhile, to make the dressing place the oil, vinegar and seasoning in a bowl or screw-top jar. Shake or mix thoroughly to combine. Place the cucumber, tomatoes, onion and olives in a bowl.

3 Break the bread into chunks and add to the bowl with the basil. Pour the dressing over the salad, and toss before serving.

ingredients

500g/1¼lb **Jerusalem artichokes**
pared **rind** and **juice** of 1 **lemon**
1 large **radicchio** or 150g/5oz radicchio leaves
40g/1½oz/6 tbsp **walnut** pieces
45ml/3 tbsp **walnut oil**
coarse **sea salt** and ground **black pepper**
flat leaf **parsley**, to garnish (optional)

radicchio, artichoke & walnut salad

THE **DISTINCTIVE**, EARTHY TASTE OF JERUSALEM ARTICHOKES MAKES A LOVELY **CONTRAST** TO THE SHARP **FRESHNESS** OF RADICCHIO AND LEMON. SERVE WARM OR COLD – EITHER IS **DELICIOUS**.

method
SERVES 4

1 Peel the artichokes and cut up any large ones so the pieces are all roughly the same size. Add the artichokes to a pan of boiling salted water with half the lemon juice and cook for 5–7 minutes until tender. Drain. Preheat the grill to high.

2 Combine the radicchio and walnuts in a heatproof bowl. Add the walnut oil and toss to coat.

3 Toss the artichokes into the salad with the remaining lemon juice and the pared rind. Season with coarse salt and pepper. Grill until beginning to brown. Serve at once, garnished with torn pieces of parsley, if you like.

roasted tomato & mozzarella salad

ROASTING THE TOMATOES ADDS A **NEW** DIMENSION TO THIS SALAD. MAKE THE BASIL OIL JUST BEFORE SERVING TO RETAIN ITS **FRESH FLAVOUR** AND VIVID COLOUR.

method

SERVES 4

1 Preheat the oven to 200°C/400°F/Gas 6 and oil a baking sheet. Cut the tomatoes in half lengthways and remove the seeds. Place skin-side down on the baking sheet and roast for 20 minutes or until the tomatoes are tender but still retain their shape.

2 Meanwhile, make the basil oil. Place the basil leaves, olive oil and garlic in a food processor or blender and process until smooth. Transfer to a bowl and chill until required.

3 For each serving, place the tomato halves on top of 2 or 3 slices of mozzarella and drizzle over the basil oil. Season well. Garnish with basil leaves and serve at once.

ingredients

olive oil, for brushing

6 large plum **tomatoes**

2 balls fresh **mozzarella cheese,** cut into 8–12 slices

salt and freshly ground **black pepper**

basil leaves, to garnish

For the basil oil

25 **basil** leaves

60ml/4 tbsp extra virgin **olive oil**

1 **garlic** clove, crushed

tuna & bean salad

THIS **SUBSTANTIAL** SALAD MAKES A GOOD ANTIPASTO, AND CAN BE VERY **QUICKLY ASSEMBLED** FROM CANNED INGREDIENTS.

method

SERVES 4-6

1 Pour the beans into a large strainer and rinse under cold water. Drain well. Place in a serving dish.

2 Break the tuna into fairly large flakes and arrange over the beans.

3 In a small bowl make the dressing by combining the oil with the lemon juice. Season with salt and pepper, and stir in the parsley. Mix well. Pour over the beans and tuna.

4 Sprinkle with the spring onions. Toss well before serving and garnish with parsley sprigs.

ingredients

2 x 400g/14oz cans **cannellini or borlotti beans**

2 x 200g/7oz cans **tuna fish,** drained

60ml/4 tbsp extra virgin **olive oil**

30ml/2 tbsp fresh **lemon juice**

15ml/1 tbsp chopped fresh **parsley**, plus extra sprigs to serve

3 **spring onions**, thinly sliced

salt and ground **black pepper**

ingredients

450g/1lb prepared **squid**, cut
    into rings
4 **garlic** cloves, roughly chopped
300ml/½pint/1¼ cups Italian
    red wine
450g/1lb waxy **new potatoes,**
    scrubbed clean
225g/8oz **French beans**,
    trimmed and cut into short
    lengths
2–3 **sun-dried tomatoes** in oil,
    drained and thinly sliced
    lengthways
60ml/4tbsp extra virgin
    olive oil
15ml/1 tbsp **red wine vinegar**
salt and ground
    black pepper

genoese squid salad

THIS IS A **GOOD SALAD** FOR SUMMER, WHEN FRENCH BEANS AND NEW POTATOES ARE AT THEIR **BEST**.

method

SERVES 4-6

1 Preheat the oven to 180ºC/350ºF/Gas 4. Put the squid rings in an heatproof dish with half the garlic, the wine and pepper to taste. Cover and cook for 45 minutes or until the squid is tender.

2 Put the potatoes in a saucepan, cover with cold water and add a good pinch of salt. Bring to the boil, cover and simmer for 15–20 minutes or until tender. Using a draining spoon, lift out the potatoes and set aside. Add the beans to the boiling water and cook for 3 minutes. Drain.

3 When the potatoes are cool enough to handle, slice them thickly on the diagonal and place them in a bowl with the warm beans and sun-dried tomatoes. Whisk the oil, wine vinegar and the remaining garlic in a jug and add salt and pepper to taste. Pour over the potato mixture.

4 Drain the squid and discard the wine and garlic. Add the squid to the potato mixture and fold very gently to mix. Arrange the salad on individual plates and grind pepper liberally all over. Serve warm.

cook's tip
The French potato called Charlotte is perfect for this type of salad because it retains its shape and does not break up when boiled. Prepared squid can be bought from supermarkets with fresh fish counters, and from fishmongers.

ingredients

1 **red pepper**

1 **yellow pepper**

4 **sun-dried tomatoes** in oil,
  drained

4 ripe **plum tomatoes**, sliced

2 canned **anchovies,** drained
  and chopped

15ml/1 tbsp **capers**, drained

15ml/1 tbsp **pine nuts**

1 **garlic** clove, very thinly sliced

For the dressing

75ml/5 tbsp extra virgin **olive oil**

15ml/1 tbsp **balsamic vinegar**

5ml/1 tsp **lemon juice**

chopped fresh **mixed herbs**

salt and ground **black pepper**

roasted pepper salad

THIS IS A SICILIAN-STYLE SALAD, USING
SOME TYPICAL INGREDIENTS FROM THE
ITALIAN ISLAND. THE **FLAVOUR** IMPROVES IF
THE SALAD IS MADE AND **DRESSED** AN HOUR
OR TWO BEFORE **SERVING.**

method

SERVES 4

1 Preheat a hot grill. Cut the peppers in half, and remove the seeds and
stalks. Cut into quarters and grill, skin side up, until the skin chars.
Transfer to a bowl, and cover with a plate. Leave to cool. Peel the
peppers and cut into strips.

2 Thinly slice the sun-dried tomatoes. Arrange the peppers and fresh
tomatoes in a serving dish. Scatter over the chopped anchovies,
sun-dried tomatoes, capers, pine nuts and garlic.

3 To make the dressing, mix together the olive oil, vinegar, lemon juice
and chopped herbs and season with salt and pepper. Pour over the
salad, distributing the dressing evenly.

salad leaves with gorgonzola

CRISPY FRIED PANCETTA MAKES **TASTY** CROUTONS, WHICH **CONTRAST** WELL IN TEXTURE AND **FLAVOUR** WITH THE SOFTNESS OF MIXED SALAD LEAVES AND THE **SHARP** TASTE OF GORGONZOLA.

method

SERVES 4

1 Put the chopped pancetta and garlic in a frying pan and heat gently, stirring constantly, until the pancetta fat runs. Increase the heat and fry until crisp. Remove with a draining spoon and drain on kitchen paper. Leave the pancetta fat in the pan, off the heat.

2 Tear the rocket and radicchio leaves into a salad bowl. Sprinkle over the walnuts, pancetta and garlic. Add salt and pepper and toss to mix. Crumble the Gorgonzola on top.

3 Return the frying pan to a medium heat and add the oil and balsamic vinegar to the pancetta fat. Stir until sizzling, then pour over the salad. Serve at once, to be tossed at the table.

ingredients

225g/8oz **pancetta rashers**, rinds removed and coarsely chopped

2 large **garlic** cloves, roughly chopped

75g/3oz **rocket** leaves

75g/3oz **radicchio** leaves

50g/2oz/½ cup **walnuts**, roughly chopped

115g/4oz **Gorgonzola cheese**

60ml/4 tbsp **olive oil**

15ml/1 tbsp **balsamic vinegar**

salt and ground **black pepper**

variation
Use walnut oil instead of olive oil, or hazelnuts and hazelnut oil instead of walnuts and olive oil.

ingredients

225g/8oz **new potatoes**,
    halved if large

50g/2oz **green beans**

115g/4oz young **spinach** leaves

2 **spring onions**, sliced

4 **eggs**, hard-boiled and quartered

50g/2oz **Parma ham**,
    cut into strips

juice of ½ **lemon**

salt and ground black **pepper**

For the dressing

60ml/4 tbsp **olive oil**

5ml/1 tsp ground **turmeric**

5ml/1 tsp ground **cumin**

50g/2oz/½ cup **hazelnuts**

warm salad of parma ham

WITH A LIGHTLY SPICED **NUTTY** DRESSING, THIS WARM SALAD IS AS **DELICIOUS** AS IT IS **FASHIONABLE**, AND AN EXCELLENT CHOICE FOR **INFORMAL** ENTERTAINING.

method

SERVES 4

1 Cook the potatoes in boiling salted water for 10–15 minutes, until tender, then drain well. Cook the beans in boiling salted water for 2 minutes, then drain well.

2 Toss the potatoes and beans with the spinach and spring onions in a large bowl. Arrange the hard-boiled egg quarters on the salad and scatter the strips of ham over the top. Sprinkle with the lemon juice and season with plenty of salt and pepper.

3 Heat the dressing ingredients in a large frying pan and continue to cook, stirring frequently, until the nuts begin to turn golden. Pour the hot, nutty dressing over the salad and serve at once.

pasta salad with salami

THIS SALAD IS **SIMPLE** TO MAKE AND IT CAN BE PREPARED IN ADVANCE FOR A **PERFECT** STARTER.

method

1 Cook the pasta in a large saucepan of boiling salted water for about 12 minutes or according to the packet instructions, until tender but not soft. Drain and rinse with cold water, then drain again.

2 Drain the peppers and reserve 60ml/4 tbsp of the oil for the dressing. Cut the peppers into long fine strips and mix them with the olives, tomatoes and Roquefort in a large bowl. Stir in the pasta and peppered salami.

3 Divide the salad leaves among 4 bowls and spoon the pasta salad on top. Whisk the reserved oil with the vinegar, oregano, garlic and seasoning to taste. Spoon this dressing over the salad and serve at once.

ingredients

225g/8oz **pasta twists**

275g/10oz jar **charcoal-roasted peppers** in oil

115g/4oz/1 cup stoned **black olives**

4 **sun-dried tomatoes**, quartered

115g/4oz **Roquefort cheese**, crumbled

10 **peppered salami** slices, cut into strips

115g/4oz packet Continental **four-leaf salad**

30ml/2 tbsp **white wine vinegar**

30ml/2 tbsp chopped fresh **oregano**

2 **garlic** cloves, crushed

salt and ground **black pepper**

soups

ingredients

75ml/5 tbsp **olive oil**

2 large **onions**, chopped

1 **celery stick**, chopped

1 **carrot**, chopped

1 **garlic** clove, finely chopped

400g/14oz/3½ cups frozen **petit pois**

900ml/1½ pints/3¾cups **vegetable stock**

25g/1oz/1½ cup fresh **basil** leaves, roughly torn, plus extra to garnish

salt and freshly ground **black pepper**

freshly grated **Parmesan cheese**

pea &
basil soup

PLENTY OF **CRUSTY** COUNTRY BREAD IS A MUST WITH THIS **FRESH**-TASTING **SOUP**.

method

SERVES 4

1 Heat the oil in a large saucepan and add the onions, celery, carrot and garlic. Cover the pan and cook over a low heat for 45 minutes or until the vegetables are soft, stirring occasionally to prevent the vegetables from sticking.

2 Add the peas and stock to the pan and bring to the boil. Reduce the heat, add the basil and seasoning then simmer for 10 minutes.

3 Spoon the soup into a food processor or blender and process until the soup is smooth. Ladle into warm bowls, sprinkle with grated Parmesan and garnish with basil.

cream of courgette soup

THE **BEAUTY** OF THIS SOUP IS ITS **DELICATE** COLOUR, **RICH** AND **CREAMY** TEXTURE AND **SUBTLE TASTE**. IF YOU PREFER A MORE PRONOUNCED **CHEESE FLAVOUR**, USE **GORGONZOLA** INSTEAD OF **DOLCELATTE**.

method

SERVES 4–6

1 Heat the oil and butter in a large saucepan until foaming. Add the onion and cook gently until softened but not browned.

2 Add the courgettes and oregano, with salt and pepper to taste. Cook over a medium heat for 10 minutes, stirring frequently.

3 Pour in the stock and bring to the boil, stirring. Lower the heat, half cover the pan and simmer gently, stirring occasionally, for about 30 minutes. Stir in the diced Dolcelatte until melted.

4 Process the soup in a blender or food processor until smooth, then press through a sieve into a clean pan.

5 Add two-thirds of the cream and stir over a low heat until hot, but not boiling. Check the consistency and add more stock if the soup is too thick. Taste for seasoning, then pour into warmed bowls. Swirl in the remaining cream. Garnish with oregano and extra cheese and serve.

ingredients

30ml/2 tbsp **olive oil**

15g/½oz/1 tbsp **butter**

1 **onion**, roughly chopped

900g/2lb **courgettes**, trimmed and sliced

5ml/1 tsp dried **oregano**

about 600ml/1 pint/2½ cups **vegetable** or **chicken stock**, plus extra if required

115g/4oz **Dolcelatte cheese**, rind removed, diced

300ml/½ pint/1¼ cups **single cream**

salt and ground **black pepper**

fresh **oregano** and extra **Dolcelatte**, to garnish

cook's tip

To save time, trim off and discard the ends of the courgettes, cut them into thirds, then chop in a food processor fitted with the metal blade.

ingredients

90ml/6 tbsp **olive oil**

small piece of **dried chilli**,
  crumbled (optional)

175g/6oz **stale bread**, cut into
  2.5cm/1in cubes

1 **onion**, finely chopped

2 **garlic** cloves, finely chopped

675g/1½lb **ripe tomatoes**,
  peeled and chopped, or 2 x
  400g/14oz cans peeled **plum
  tomatoes**, chopped

45ml/3 tbsp chopped fresh **basil**

1.5litres/2½ pints/6¼ cups light
  meat stock or **water**, or a
  combination of both

salt and ground
  black pepper

extra virgin olive oil, to serve
  (optional)

tomato & bread soup

THIS **FLORENTINE** RECIPE WAS CREATED TO
USE UP **STALE** BREAD. IT CAN BE MADE WITH
FRESH OR CANNED **PLUM TOMATOES**.

method

SERVES 4

1 Heat 60ml/4 tbsp of the oil in a large saucepan. Add the chilli, if
using, and stir for 1–2 minutes. Add the bread cubes and cook until
golden. Remove to a kitchen-paper lined plate and drain.

2 Add the remaining oil, the onion and garlic, and cook until the onion
softens. Stir in the tomatoes, bread and basil. Season with salt. Cook
over a moderate heat, stirring occasionally, for about 15 minutes.

3 Meanwhile, heat the stock or water to simmering. Add it to the
saucepan with the tomato mixture, and mix well. Bring to the boil.
Lower the heat slightly and simmer for 20 minutes.

4 Remove the soup from the heat. Use a fork to mash the tomatoes and
the bread together. Season with pepper, and more salt if necessary.
Allow to stand for 10 minutes. Just before serving swirl in a little extra
virgin olive oil, if desired.

chilled asparagus soup

MAKE THIS DELICIOUS SOUP WHEN
ASPARAGUS IS IN SEASON AND PLENTIFUL,
USING REALLY TENDER, SLIM SPEARS.

method

SERVES 6

1 Cut the top 6cm/2½in off the asparagus spears. Blanch these tips in boiling water for 5–6 minutes or until they are just tender. Drain. Cut each tip into 2 or 3 pieces, and set aside.

2 Trim the ends of the stalks, removing any brown or woody parts. Chop the stalks into 1cm/½in pieces.

3 Heat the butter or oil in a heavy saucepan. Add the leeks or spring onions and cook over a low heat for 5–8 minutes, or until softened. Stir in the asparagus stalks, cover and cook for 6–8 minutes more.

4 Add the flour and stir well to blend. Cook for 3–4 minutes, uncovered, stirring occasionally.

5 Add the stock or water and bring to the boil, stirring frequently, then reduce the heat and simmer for 30 minutes. Season with salt and pepper.

6 Purée the soup in a food processor or blender mill. If necessary, strain it to remove any coarse fibres. Stir in the asparagus tips, most of the cream or yogurt, and the herbs. Chill well. Stir thoroughly before serving, and check the seasoning. Garnish with swirled cream or yogurt.

ingredients

900g/2lbfresh **asparagus**
50g/2oz/¼ cup **butter** or
   60ml/4 tbsp **olive oil**
350g/12oz/3 cups sliced **leeks**
   or **spring onions**
40g/1½oz/⅓ cup **plain flour**
1.5 litres/2½ pints /6¼ cups
   chicken stock or **water**
120ml/4fl oz/½ cup **single**
   cream or **natural yogurt**
15ml/1 tbsp minced fresh
   tarragon or **chervil**
salt and ground **black pepper**

ingredients

15ml/1 tbsp **olive oil**

25g/1oz/2 tbsp **butter**

1 **onion**, finely chopped

900g/2lb ripe **Italian plum
    tomatoes**, roughly chopped

1 **garlic** clove, roughly chopped

about 750ml/1¼ pints/3 cups
    chicken or **vegetable
    stock**, plus extra if required

120ml/4fl oz/½ cup **dry
    white wine**

30ml/2 tbsp **sun-dried
    tomato paste**

30ml/2 tbsp shredded fresh
    basil, plus a few whole leaves,
    to garnish

150ml/¼ pint/⅔ cup
    double cream

salt and ground
    black pepper

tomato & fresh basil soup

THIS IS A DELICIOUS **SOUP** FOR **LATE SUMMER** WHEN FRESH **TOMATOES** ARE AT THEIR MOST FLAVOURSOME.

method

SERVES 4–6

1 Heat the oil and butter in a large saucepan until foaming. Add the onion and cook gently for about 5 minutes, stirring frequently, until softened but not brown.

2 Stir in the chopped tomatoes and garlic, then add the stock, white wine and sun-dried tomato paste, with salt and pepper to taste. Bring to the boil, then lower the heat, half cover the pan and simmer gently for 20 minutes, stirring occasionally to stop the tomatoes sticking to the base of the pan.

3 Process the soup with the shredded basil in a blender or food processor, then press through a sieve into a clean pan.

4 Add the double cream and heat through, stirring. Do not allow the soup to approach boiling point. Check the consistency and add more stock if necessary and then taste for seasoning. Pour into warmed bowls and garnish with basil. Serve at once.

variation
The soup can also be served chilled. Pour it into a container after sieving and leave to cool then chill for at least 4 hours. Serve in chilled bowls.

tiny pasta in broth

THIS SOUP MAKES A SATISFYING STARTER
AND IS A GOOD WINTER WARMER TOO.

method

SERVES 4

1 Bring the beef stock to the boil in a large saucepan. Add salt and
pepper to taste, then drop in the dried soup pasta. Stir well and bring
the stock back to the boil.

2 Lower the heat to a simmer and cook until the pasta is *al dente*: 7–8
minutes or according to the instructions on the packet. Stir frequently
during the cooking to prevent the pasta shapes from sticking together.

3 Drain the pieces of roasted pepper and dice them finely. Place them in
the base of four warmed soup plates. Taste the soup for seasoning.
Ladle into the soup plates and serve immediately, with shavings of
Parmesan handed separately.

---

variation
You can use other dried tiny soup pastas in place of the funghetti.

---

ingredients

1.2 litres/2 pints/5 cups
  beef stock
75g/3oz/¾ cup dried **tiny soup
  pasta**, e.g. **funghetti**
2 pieces **bottled roasted red
  pepper**, about 50g/2oz
salt and freshly ground
  black pepper
coarsly shaved **Parmesan
  cheese**, to serve

ingredients

1 **onion**

2 **celery** sticks

1 large **carrot**

45ml/3 tbsp **olive oil**

150g/5oz **French beans**, cut
  into 5cm/2in pieces

1 **courgette**, thinly sliced

1 **potato,** cut into 1cm/½in cubes

¼ **Savoy cabbage**, shredded

1 small **aubergine**, cut
  into 1cm/½in cubes

200g/7oz can **cannellini
  beans**, drained and rinsed

2 **Italian plum
  tomatoes**, chopped

1.2 litres/2 pints/5 cups
  vegetable stock

90g/3½oz dried **spaghetti**
  or **vermicelli**

salt and ground **black pepper**

For the pesto

about 20 fresh **basil** leaves

1 **garlic** clove

10ml/2 tsp **pine nuts**

15ml/1 tbsp freshly grated
  Parmesan cheese

15ml/1 tbsp freshly grated
  Pecorino cheese

30ml/2 tbsp **olive oil**

genoese minestrone

IN **GENOA** THEY OFTEN MAKE **MINESTRONE** LIKE THIS, WITH **PESTO** STIRRED IN TOWARDS THE END OF **COOKING**. IT IS PACKED FULL OF **VEGETABLES** AND HAS A GOOD **STRONG FLAVOUR**. THERE IS **PARMESAN** CHEESE IN THE **PESTO**, SO THERE IS NO NEED TO SERVE EXTRA WITH THE SOUP.

method

SERVES 6

1 Chop the onion, celery and carrot finely. Heat the oil in a saucepan and cook over a low heat, stirring frequently, for 5–7 minutes.

2 Mix in the French beans, courgette, potato and cabbage. Stir-fry over a medium heat for about 3 minutes. Add the aubergine, cannellini beans and tomatoes, and stir-fry for 2–3 minutes more. Pour in the stock with salt and pepper to taste. Bring to the boil. Stir well, cover and lower the heat. Simmer for 40 minutes, stirring occasionally.

3 Meanwhile, process all the pesto ingredients in a food processor until the mixture forms a smooth sauce, adding water if necessary.

4 Break the pasta into small pieces and add it to the soup. Simmer, stirring frequently, for 5 minutes. Add the pesto sauce and stir it in well, then simmer for 2–3 minutes more, or until the pasta is *al dente*. Taste for seasoning. Serve hot, in warmed soup plates or bowls.

ingredients

25g/1oz/½ cup dried
  porcini mushrooms
30ml/2 tbsp **olive oil**
15g/½oz/1 tbsp **butter**
2 **leeks**, thinly sliced
2 **shallots**, roughly chopped
1 **garlic** clove, roughly chopped
225g/8oz/3 cups fresh
  wild mushrooms
about 1.2 litres/2 pints/
  5 cups **beef stock**, plus extra
  if required
2.5ml/½ tsp dried **thyme**
150ml/¼ pint/⅔ cup
  double cream
salt and ground
  black pepper
thyme sprigs, to garnish

---

cook's tip
Porcini are ceps. Italian cooks would
make this soup with a combination of
fresh and dried ceps, but if fresh
ceps are difficult to obtain, you can
use other wild mushrooms, such as
chanterelles.

wild mushroom soup

WILD **MUSHROOMS** ARE **EXPENSIVE**. BUT
AS DRIED **PORCINI** HAVE AN **INTENSE**
FLAVOUR, ONLY A **SMALL** QUANTITY IS
NEEDED. THE **BEEF STOCK** MAY SEEM
UNUSUAL IN A VEGETABLE SOUP, BUT IT
HELPS TO **STRENGTHEN** THE EARTHY
FLAVOUR OF THE MUSHROOMS.

method   SERVES 4

1 Put the dried porcini in a bowl, add 250ml/8fl oz/1 cup warm water
and leave to soak for 20–30 minutes.

2 Lift out of the liquid and squeeze over the bowl to remove as much of
the soaking liquid as possible. Strain all the liquid and reserve to use
later. Finely chop the porcini.

3 Heat the oil and butter in a large saucepan until foaming. Add the
sliced leeks, chopped shallots and garlic, and cook gently for about
5 minutes, stirring frequently, until softened but not coloured.

4 Chop or slice the fresh mushrooms and add to the pan. Stir over a
medium heat for a few minutes until they begin to soften. Pour in the
stock and bring to the boil. Add the porcini, soaking liquid, dried
thyme and salt and pepper. Lower the heat, half cover the pan and
simmer gently for 30 minutes, stirring occasionally.

5 Pour about three-quarters of the soup into a blender or food
processor and process until smooth. Return to the soup remaining in
the pan, stir in the cream and heat through. Check the consistency
and add more stock if the soup is too thick. Taste for seasoning.
Serve hot, garnished with thyme sprigs.

ingredients

350g/12oz/1½ cups **dried**
   cannellini or other
   white beans
1 **bay** leaf
75ml/5 tbsp **olive oil**
1 **onion**, finely chopped
1 **carrot**, finely chopped
1 **celery** stick, finely chopped
3 **tomatoes**, peeled and
   finely chopped
2 **garlic** cloves, finely chopped
5ml/1 tsp fresh **thyme** leaves, or
   2.5ml/½ tsp dried thyme
750ml/1¼ pints/3 cups
   boiling **water**
salt and ground
   black pepper
extra virgin olive oil, to serve

white bean soup

A THICK **PURÉE** OF COOKED **DRIED** BEANS IS
AT THE **HEART** OF THIS **SUBSTANTIAL**
COUNTRY SOUP FROM **TUSCANY**. IT MAKES A
WARMING WINTER ANTIPASTO.

method

SERVES 6

1 Soak the beans in a large bowl of cold water overnight. Drain. Place
the beans in a large saucepan of water, bring to the boil, and cook for
20 minutes. Drain. Return the beans to the pan, cover with cold water,
and bring to the boil again.

2 Add the bay leaf and cook until the beans are tender, 1–2 hours.
Drain again. Remove the bay leaf.

3 Purée about three-quarters of the beans in a food processor, or pass
through a food mill, adding a little water if necessary.

4 Heat the oil in a large saucepan. Stir in the onion, and cook until it
softens. Add the carrot and celery and cook for 5 minutes more.

5 Stir in the tomatoes, garlic and thyme. Cook for 6–8 minutes more,
stirring often.

6 Pour in the boiling water. Stir in the beans and the bean purée.
Season with salt and pepper. Simmer for 10–15 minutes. Serve in
individual soup bowls, sprinkled with a little extra virgin olive oil.

borlotti bean & pasta soup

THIS IS A **VERSION** OF A CLASSIC **ITALIAN SOUP**. TRADITIONALLY, THE PERSON WHO FINDS THE **BAY LEAF** IS HONOURED WITH A **KISS** FROM THE COOK.

method

SERVES 4

1 Place the chopped onion, celery and carrots in a large saucepan with the olive oil. Cook over a medium heat for 5 minutes or until the vegetables soften, stirring occasionally.

2 Add the bay leaf, wine, if using, stock and tomatoes and bring to the boil. Reduce the heat and simmer for 10 minutes until the vegetables are just tender.

3 Add the pasta and beans and bring the soup back to the boil, then simmer for 8 minutes until the pasta is *al dente*. Stir frequently to prevent the pasta sticking.

4 Season to taste, add the spinach and cook for a further 2 minutes. Serve, sprinkled with grated Parmesan cheese.

---

cook's tip

Other pulses, such as cannellini beans, haricot beans or chick-peas, are equally good in this soup.

---

ingredients

1 **onion**, chopped

1 **celery** stick, chopped

2 **carrots**, chopped

75ml/5 tbsp **olive oil**

1 **bay** leaf

1 glass **white wine** (optional)

1.2 litres/2 pints/5 cups **vegetables stock**

400g/14oz/3 cups canned chopped **tomatoes**

175g/6oz/1½ cups **pasta shapes**, e.g. **farfalle** or **conchiglie**

400g/14oz/3 cups canned **borlotti beans**, drained

250g/9oz **spinach**, washed and thick stalks removed

salt and freshly ground **black pepper**

50g/2oz/⅔ cup grated **Parmesan cheese**, to serve

ingredients

675g/1½lb fresh
spinach, washed

45ml/3 tbsp **extra virgin
olive oil**

1 small **onion**, finely chopped

2 **garlic** cloves, finely chopped

1 small fresh **red chilli**, seeded
and finely chopped

115g/4oz/generous 1 cup
risotto rice

1.2 litres/2 pints/5 cups
vegetable stock

60ml/4 tbsp grated
Pecorino cheese

salt and ground
black pepper

spinach &
rice soup

USE VERY **FRESH**, YOUNG **SPINACH LEAVES**
TO PREPARE THIS **LIGHT** AND FRESH-
TASTING SOUP.

method   SERVES 4

1 Place the spinach in a large pan with just the water that clings to its
leaves after washing. Add a large pinch of salt.

2 Heat gently until the spinach has wilted, then remove from the heat
and drain, reserving any liquid.

3 Either chop the spinach finely using a large knife or place in a food
processor and process to a fairly coarse purée.

4 Heat the oil in a large saucepan and gently cook the onion, garlic and
chilli for 4–5 minutes until softened. Stir in the rice until well coated,
then pour in the stock and reserved spinach liquid. Bring to the boil,
lower the heat and simmer for 10 minutes. Add the spinach, with salt
and pepper to taste. Cook for 5–7 minutes more, until the rice is
tender. Check the seasoning and serve with the Pecorino cheese.

baby carrot & fennel soup

SWEET **TENDER** CARROTS FIND THEIR MOMENT OF **GLORY** IN THIS DELICATELY **SPICED SOUP**. FENNEL PROVIDES AN ANISEED **FLAVOUR** WITHOUT **OVERPOWERING** THE CARROTS.

method

SERVES 4

1 Melt the butter in a large saucepan and add the spring onions, fennel, celery, carrots and cumin. Cover and cook for 5 minutes until soft.

2 Add the potatoes and stock, and simmer for a further 10 minutes.

3 Liquidize the mixture in the pan with a hand-held blender. Stir in the cream and season to taste. Serve in individual bowls and garnish with chopped fresh parsley.

ingredients

50g/2oz/¼ cup **butter**

1 small bunch **spring onions**, chopped

150g/5oz **fennel** bulb, chopped

1 **celery** stick, chopped

450g/1lb new **carrots**, grated

2.5ml/½ tsp ground **cumin**

150g/5oz **new potatoes**, peeled and diced

1.2 litres/2 pints/5 cups **chicken** or **vegetable stock**

60ml/4 tbsp **double cream**

salt and ground **black pepper**

60ml/4 tbsp chopped fresh **parsley**, to garnish

cook's tip
For convenience, you can freeze the soup in portions before adding the cream, seasoning and parsley.

index